Not Your Turn

Is there a greater purpose for our lives?

COPYRIGHT

© 2019 Jay Armstrong

This work is protected by US Copyright law. Unauthorized duplication or distribution without the author's express written consent is strictly prohibited.

ISBN 13: 978-0-9906039-5-5 (Kettlebell Club)

DEDICATION

I wish I had learned more about the lives of my relatives and ancestors when I had the chance. I am especially disappointed that I did not ask more questions of my mother and father. What mistakes did they make? Where did they grow up? Who were their friends? What jobs did they have?

Rather than continuing to beat myself up about this I decided to help my children know a little more about their father. In this book, I choose to do this by sharing some near-death or life-changing events that I clearly remember.

There are certainly many more days that were less exciting – days of hard work or play. But, I found these stories particularly interesting and hope you will also enjoy them.

This book is dedicated to Jayka and Itusik.

FOREWARD

I played in a rock band for several years with a talented, young keyboard player, Chris Bailey. I attended high school for a couple of years with Chris' younger sister, Renee Bailey. Renee was a ballet dancer who worked with me in a high school production of Camelot. Renee later went on to dance with the American Ballet Theater.

Chris and Renee had a younger sister, Michelle. Michelle and I dated for several years. Michelle was also a ballet dancer who danced with the New York City Ballet. Obviously, this was a talented group of young people. Michelle's family lived in a broad, ranch-style home on several acres of land in Alvin, Texas. Things were going well for all of them. But, fate had a surprise waiting.

Michelle had taken a few months off from dancing and was temporarily living with her parents. Her father had recently completed a continuing education course in Spanish was attended a graduation ceremony with Michelle and her mother on the west side of town.

They drove home on Highway 6 through Manvel, Texas where I had lived while attending high school. At the exact same time, a car with two teenaged boys and two teenaged girls was traveling along County Road 99. These two roads form a "T" where County Road 99 terminates into Highway 6.

The Baileys were traveling on Highway 6 at approximately 65 miles per hour heading toward their Alvin home. The teenagers were traveling at a 90-degree angle at about 100 miles per hour. The teenagers didn't slow down for the stop sign at Highway 6 and the Baileys apparently never saw them coming. The teenagers' car hit the Baileys' car in the center of the driver's door. Everyone involved in this two-car incident died.

The loss of several people who were very close to me still stings. The memory often climbs to the surface from my subconscious and I feel great sadness for the loss. Michelle and her parents died and left behind a shattered family of Chris, Renee, and three other young boys.

I like to think of myself as a logical guy. I studied physics and engineering in college. It seems to me that it would be virtually impossible to have two cars traveling at such high rates of speed approach each other at a 90-degree angle and succeed in running into each other in such a precise and catastrophic manner.

I don't know if this is fate, coincidence, or the will of God, but it seems that similar forces of mysterious events have been at work throughout my life. I have had numerous events that could have ended my life or certainly would have radically altered the path of my journey.

So, the purpose of this book is to share a few interesting tales from my life's journey as though we were sitting around a campfire. Some of the tales, in retrospect, may seem quite amusing. Perhaps these tales will remind you of some extraordinary moments that have occurred in your life.

Another purpose of this book is to hopefully stimulate your curiosity. I have been asking myself for many years, "Why am I still here?" Don't get me wrong. I am not in a hurry to depart. But it seems that I have had many high-probability opportunities for the Grim Reaper to tap on my shoulder. I now believe that any life well-lived or filled with success must include some good luck, a positive destiny, fortuitous fate, or a higher power.

After reading these stories, perhaps you, too, will ask yourself, "Why am I still here?" Perhaps it is not yet your turn.

A Life Well Lived	9
Does God Exist?	10
Story 1 – Allergies (c. 1957)	11
Story 2 – I Want to Play, Too! (c. 1961)	13
Story 3 – Finding Firewood (c. 1963)	15
Story 4 – Back of the Truck (c. 1967)	18
Story 5 – Gravity (c. 1968)	20
Story 6 – It's Bailey's Turn (c. 1971)	23
Story 7 – A Girl and a Shoulder (c. 1973)	25
Story 8 – Magic Bed (c. 1974)	27
Story 9 – Extra Pay (1975)	30
Story 10 – Gone in Five Seconds (1978)	33
Story 11 – Did Alice Do This? (1981)	35
Story 12 – It is a Classic (1982)	38
Story 13 – Misfire (c. 1983)	40
Story 14 – Abandon Ship (c. 1983)	42
Story 15 – A Wrench in the Works (c. 1984)	44
Story 16 - On the Runway (c. 1986)	47
Story 17 - Close the Business (c. 1987)	52
Story 18 - Road Rally (c. 1988)	55
Story 19 - Change Lanes (c. 1989)	57
Story 20 – Mountain Surprise (1999)	60
Story 21 – Big Toe (c. 2002)	65
Story 22 - Alternate Route (2002)	68
Story 23 - Merry Christmas (2003)	72
Story 24 – Stand Up (2015)	75
One More Story	78
Epilogue	83
It Doesn't Matter	83
Paradigm	84
Suffering	85
Lessons	85
Society	86

Family	87
Children	88
Love	89

A Life Well Lived

I have spent much time thinking about my life and the lives of others. Sometimes I think I have it all figured out. When I am in one of these particularly self-congratulatory moods, this is what I perceive to be the usual pattern:

- We are born.
- We grow up and obtain an education.
- We go to work, acquire possessions, and raise a family.
- We reach old age and retire.
- We die and make room for the younger generations.

If all things go according to plan we will have a positive impact on this world and the people in it and we will leave the world a little better off than it was on our arrival. We will work and play. We will love others and there will be a few people who love us and who will miss us when we are gone.

But, this seems somehow inadequate. I am certain that I am not the first person to ask myself, "Why are we all doing this?" In fact, most of us question the meaning of life and we do this often through out our lives. Our reason for getting up each day and pursuing our activities with zeal changes throughout the seasons of our lives. As teenagers and young adults the hormones raging in our bodies cause us to spend much of our time hunting for an appropriate companion. These same hormones give us additional energy we can use to aggressively pursue education, careers, and other activities.

As we age we may want to insure our security so as not to be a burden on others. Or, perhaps we will want to give back something to our community, our descendants, and to others we love. We might also become more introspective and want to write stories of our lives so that others can learn from our mistakes or gain from our wisdom. Hopefully, we will live life with few regrets and have some great stories to tell.

Does God Exist?

This book is a collection of stories often involving coincidences or close calls. These events make me wonder if God has had a hand in controlling them so that my existence continued. I am not trying to convince you that God exists. There is an ample supply of religious leaders with whom you can consult on this matter and texts you can read. And, at least in this book, I do not plan to lay out all of my religious and spiritual beliefs and the lengthy path I took to develop them.

Even though I was raised in the Lutheran church and went to a private, religious school I have always been skeptical of all religious beliefs including my own. It has always been easier for me to find solace in mathematics, geometric concepts and logic. So, this book is about patterns.

For example, it is certainly *possible* to win the lottery once per year for ten years. It is, however *very* unlikely. In fact, if you were to achieve this feat, the entire world would probably seek you out and try to learn how you did it. *No one* would believe it was purely luck.

This is the kind of luck I am talking about! Love, conception, fertilization, and birth comprise the miracle of life. But, the fact that I am still alive, I didn't end up in prison, and I am not seriously disfigured is, to my way of thinking, an equally inexplicable event. Not only must I ask myself, "Why am I here?" But, I must also ask myself, "Why am I *still* here?"

Join me as we take a look at a few moments of my life. These are often moments when, except for a split second of time, the distance of a millimeter, or the luck of the draw, my life could have turned out quite a bit differently.

Story 1 – Allergies (c. 1957)

I was born the fourth child to Sonny and Frances Armstrong. They were strong people and they were survivors.

My father served in the military during World War II. Miraculously, he was still standing after the assault on Okinawa. It is estimated that 50,000 Allied troops and 100,000 Japanese died in this three-month long campaign of spring and early summer of 1945. His first child was a daughter named Linda. She was born while he was fighting in the Pacific.

Lawrence "Sonny" Armstrong, Pfc (c. 1943)

In 1953, only a few years before I was born, Sonny and Frances' second child, Laura, died from cancer. Of course, infant mortality was much higher in previous generations, but death of a child by cancer was no doubt a heavy weight for them to bear. My parents had therefore already been through quite a bit of stress and worry about life and their children before I even showed up. It seems that my days as an infant further continued their anxiety.

As a baby, I developed a rash, had trouble breathing and began losing weight. These are not good things for an infant. The doctors determined that I was allergic to milk. This was many years ago and it took a while to figure this out. I ended up in the hospital. I had significant swelling and, according to my mother, they had numerous IVs and tubes stuck in me. Finally, they put me on a soy-based formula and I recovered. Apparently, this period was traumatic enough for my mother to describe it to me many, many times.

Of course, I don't remember this. By the time I was a small child I was eating cereal most mornings with regular, whole milk on it. And, as a teenager, I regularly drank many glasses of the stuff.

While still an infant (or perhaps a toddler), I became ill again. This time it was with some kind of sinus or ear infection. The concerned parents took me to the family doctor, Dr. Joseph T. Ainsworth. I recall his name because he was our doctor for many years and for most of my childhood years I was certain I would grow up to be a doctor.

To help cure the raging infection, Dr. Ainsworth prescribed a round of penicillin, one of the few antibiotics available at the time. This turned out to be a bad thing for me. Apparently, I am highly allergic to penicillin. Once again I was rushed to the hospital as I began to swell and have trouble breathing. Mom usually cried when she told me this story. She said they had more tubes and needles stuck in me in every available location. They were unsure whether or not I would survive.

But, through the miracles of science or a baby's will to survive, I recovered. Now, although I continue to avoid penicillin, it seems my worst allergy is to the mold and pollen in spring and fall seasons.

Story 2 – I Want to Play, Too! (c. 1961)

Many of my relatives lived near Denver, Colorado when I was a child. Mom and Dad used to pack up the car with luggage and kids and make the lengthy drive across Texas and New Mexico to visit them.

The road trip from Houston to Denver always took two days. Mom and Dad both smoked in the car so it was very difficult for us to breathe. We played every game we could think of. There were no movies or video games to play. We tried to sleep by lying on the floor and up on the deck near the rear window. In those days, no one wore seat belts. Mom and dad would be drinking beer for most of the trip. Things have definitely changed a bit over the past five decades.

When we arrived in Colorado we stayed with my mother's sister, Deede, and her family in their small home in the countryside. Deede and her husband, Ed, raised chickens, rabbits and a couple of cows on the land behind their home.

My brother, Tom, and I would go bird hunting in the hills and trees in the surrounding area. This was an untamed area with lots of rocks, cacti and hills. There were boundless opportunities to have fun and get exercise. Of course, there were also many ways to get hurt.

One day, my brother, Tom, and our cousin, Larry, were playing outside. I am five years younger than Tom and the other boys were clearly uninterested in having me tag along. At the time I was five years old. They could move faster and climb better than me. This meant that I tried even harder to include myself in their activities.

Tom and Larry climbed the steep hill behind the house. I followed the boys from the chicken yard into the area that was fenced off for the calf. Then I climbed upon the rickety barbed wire fence that was barely supported by a few old tree branches that served as fence posts. The old barbed wire was wrapped around the pieces of wood and almost completely rusted through in places. As I tried to climb this poorly constructed fence, my feet became tangled in the barbed wire and I fell forward. I was unaware that I was falling toward two barrels used to provide water for the calf. These watering barrels had been made from a single 55-gallon barrel that had been cut in half with a pair of tin snips. The upward pointing edges of these rusted half-barrels were sharp and jagged. They had been outside in the elements, rusting away for many years. Mother nature was reclaiming them.

As I fell, I broke my fall by putting my right arm in front of myself. Suddenly, I was on the ground. Then, I remember my brother running back to me and asking, "Are you okay?" I could tell he was very upset and this was unusual for my brother. He was rarely concerned about whether or not I was injured. In fact, he was usually the cause of my injuries. I said, "Yes, I am fine". But, then looking down at the chicken manure-covered dirt in front of my face, I noticed there was blood seeping out from underneath my hand. I said weakly, "No, I am not okay – I am bleeding."

We made our way back to the house. Mom and Dad wrapped my hand and arm up in some old rags and off we went to the hospital. The doctor in the emergency room gave me seven stitches in the palm of my hand, ten stitches in my forearm, a tetanus shot and some antibiotics. And, just like that, we were on our way back home.

The only permanent damage was a couple of small scars. Now, it is difficult to find these remnants from the past.

This story clearly has a happy ending. But, I could easily have been facially disfigured, blinded or even incurred a fatal injury. I could have lost some function in my hand or arm. With all the feces and rust I could have acquired some horrible infection or disease. How would my life have been different with a large scar across my face or one eye? I am sure that my life's journey would have been quite different.

Story 3 – Finding Firewood (c. 1963)

My mom's younger sister, Fern, married a man named Roy. Uncle Roy was often a great guy to be around. He was energetic, funny, and played guitar with my father. He was also a trainer for the Houston professional boxing club, The Golden Gloves. He was strong and was an excellent fighter. But, he also had a mean streak. He often went out late at night to try and test his street fighting skills.

At the time of this story, I was only seven years old and I loved my uncle Roy even though I knew about the recurring trouble in Fern and Roy's home. Roy occasionally beat Fern. He used his fighting skills to mistreat her. Once, he even broke one of her ribs and caused extensive bruising all over her body.

After these incidents of abuse, Fern would come to our home. My mom would take photos of the injuries, Fern would leave Roy, and a complaint would be filed with the police. After a week or two, Roy would profess his sincere regret and promise never to abuse her again. Fern would drop all charges and return home. After all, she had to think about the children. This sad, horrible cycle was repeated over and over.

Now to my story. My family and my uncle Jim occasionally went floundering on Matagorda Island. Matagorda is one of the barrier islands off the Texas coast. In those days this island was rarely visited and was an ideal site for gigging flounders. To do this, one would walk along the shore in the darkness while carrying a lantern and a long stick with a sharp point or a "gig". In the darkness these strange flat fish, with both eyes on the same side of their heads, would come near the shore and slightly bury themselves in the sand. All that was required for success was to find the flounder lying on the mud, gig it and then pick it up. We would often bring back thirty or more flounders on such trips.

Bruners and Armstrongs with Flounder

On one such trip my uncle Roy came with us. We brought our boats ashore and began to set up camp. This involved putting up one or more tents, unpacking the food, and building a fire. There was little sleep on one of these trips so the campsite was not a very big production. The campfire was important though if only for the light it provided.

Uncle Roy and I set off to collect wood for our campfire. Most of the wood on these barrier islands is driftwood, which is not a good fuel for a campfire. But, spread out in the brush of the island one could find pieces of wood that were useful. Uncle Roy and I had been collecting wood for about an hour when he spotted a nice piece of wood resting against one of the island's bushes. As he headed toward the bush I spotted a snake coiled up in it. I shouted to uncle Roy to stop. He kept walking and calmly asked my why I was hollering. I said urgently,

"There is a snake in the bush!" Finally, he stopped and then he saw the creature I had described. As was the usual case, Roy was unafraid. He took one of the pieces of wood we had already collected and, using it, he killed the snake. It was a rattlesnake that was about seven feet long. The snake was as big around as a man's forearm and had fourteen rattles. This means it was a rather old snake.

Roy thanked me and said, "You saved my life." He cut off the rattles and gave them to me as a present. I kept these rattles for many years.

We returned home and Roy returned to his abusive ways. A few years later, Fern was diagnosed with pancreatic cancer and died. This left Roy's youngest daughter in the house. According to her, the abuse was simply transferred to her. What would have happened if I hadn't warned Roy about the snake? Perhaps some of the additional abuse inflicted on his wife and daughter could have been averted. Roy was not a nice guy yet he lived a full life. Why does life work this way?

Story 4 – Back of the Truck (c. 1967)

Mom and Dad were very good friends with our neighbors, Al and Annette. In the late 1960's we all went together to a park to camp out. We stayed in tents, played outside and generally had a great time. Al and Annette had brought along their three daughters: Robin, Lynette, and Lisa. Mom and Dad brought me, my sister, and my best friend from school, David.

After a couple of days of eating, playing and camping fun we prepared to leave. The two families had travelled to the park in separate vehicles since there were too many people to fit in a single car. My family was loaded into my Dad's 1967 blue, Chevrolet pickup truck.

In those days it was quite common for people, including children, to ride in the back of a pickup truck. In fact, seat belts had only recently been included in all vehicles and their use was strictly optional. For example, during many of our vacations to Colorado, we would lie above the seats in our car near the rear window or in the floor in front of the seats in order to sleep a little. There are nowadays many more safety laws.

David and my sister, Sunny, were riding in the back of the pickup truck with me. As we made our way to the exit of the park, David and I saw about a dozen boards lying in the back of the pickup truck. They were small boards but about six feet in length. They were probably 1x2 boards. Being creative kids, we made a deck of these boards near the cab of the truck by placing the boards across the width of the bed of the pickup. David and I sat on this deck as we began to leave the park. I could readily tell that David, who was a little bit chunky, and I combined to exceed the amount of weight that the boards could handle.

Then, my sister, Sunny, suddenly decided she wanted to move closer to her older brother. She inexplicably lay on the bed of the truck and slid underneath the inadequate platform that held two 8-year-old boys.

What made David and I decide to build an unstable platform in the back of the pickup truck? What made Sunny want to lie down under us?

I can't answer these questions, but almost as soon as she was beneath us, one of the boards snapped. I jumped off the hastily constructed deck in horror. What had just happened? I heard Sunny cry out in pain. The sharp end of the shattered board cut the side of her nose and hit her just below her left eye. There was only a little bleeding and not much more damage. I was in shock. Inspection of the broken board revealed an extremely sharp point where the yellow pine had snapped in two at a knot. Yet, the injury didn't even require stitches. How was this possible? To me, the event was miraculous. One inch to the right or one inch higher and she would have had the sharp end of a broken board hit her directly in the left eye.

I felt that I had made a poor choice by building a deck that was clearly unsafe. I had done even worse by allowing my sister to position herself in harm's way. But, mostly I felt extremely lucky to have escaped a life-changing event. How would I have felt if my sister had lost her eye due to my carelessness? How would her life been different? We would never know because it didn't turn out that way.

Story 5 – Gravity (c. 1968)

My family was certain I would grow to be more than six feet tall. They were wrong. The reason for this belief was that I grew quickly until I was eleven years old. At that time I was already 5'-10" tall. I attended a private school with few students. So, I was the tallest boy in the class. I felt like a big, important guy.

This is a story about the evil of which we are all capable and how I overestimated my strength.

There were only three boys in my class. This led to a strange social situation. At that age, we felt that we must have and identify our "best" friend. This meant that my best friend was Charlie for a week or two. Then, my best friend would be Dave. Of course, there were times when I was out of the loop and had no best friend.

One day while Dave was my best friend, we went outside to play together at class recess. One of the few things we had to play with at our small school was a tetherball. This is a pole, about 8 feet tall with a ball attached to the top by a thin rope. The one at my school had a tire filled with concrete as a base. The pole was made of pipe that was about 1-1/2" in diameter and was split into two four foot pieces that slipped together.

Tetherball

The game is designed for two players. The players stand on opposite sides and hit the ball. The objective is to wrap the rope around the pole by hitting the ball past your opponent. When the rope is completely wrapped, the game is over.

I don't recall why, but at some point I became very angry with Dave. It would not be the last time that I became angry as the result of some silly game. But, games are only interesting if we suspend reality and become thoroughly engrossed in the activity.

In this case, I became thoroughly enraged. Dave and I said hateful things to each other and then Dave started to walk away. I decided to strike out at him, literally.

I don't know why, but I pulled the top half of the pole from the tetherball, took a couple of steps toward the retreating boy whose back was toward me, and I went to strike him with it.

Then, I panicked. I yelled, "Look out!"

I did this because I realized that, as the tetherball pole started downward toward Dave's head, that this attack was going to kill him. The pole with the ball attached to the end was quite heavy and I was not going to be able to stop it on the way down.

My mind was racing. What had made me want to kill my friend? In reality, I hadn't thought this attack through thoroughly in advance. But, now I could see there must be some serious evil buried deep inside of me. I was also destined to pay a price for this horrendous attack. Perhaps I would end up in jail or some special place for wayward children. As a minimum I was going to regret this outburst of emotion.

I used all of my strength to try to stop the descent of the pole. I couldn't complete overcome gravity, but I was able to slow it down significantly. As a result of my yell, Dave turned around and moved just enough so that, rather than striking his head, it glanced off of his shoulder.

Instead of dying from a crushed skull, Dave had a painful bruise. He was very angry about the attack. I expressed my sincere remorse and asked for his forgiveness. I think he could see how upset I was at this near tragic event. We eventually put the incident behind us and remained good friends.

I imagine that many gunshot murders or attacks with knives or hammers are similar to this. One party becomes so enraged that he just doesn't think. Sincere regret follows, but it is simply too late. Fortunately for me, it is just another memory of a close call. Just another story in a book of close calls.

Story 6 – It's Bailey's Turn (c. 1971)

My parents, in an effort to provide me with morals, values and a superior education, sent me to a Lutheran school from first grade through eighth grade. The classes there were small. As a result, there were a limited number of athletes for the school's sports team.

My sixth grade teacher, Mr. Gaede, was the coach of the basketball, baseball and football teams. As soon as I was old enough to play on these teams, he set about recruiting me. I recall coming home from school and informing my parents that I wanted to play on the football team. It should be noted that at Zion Lutheran School, we did not wear pads and tackle one another. Rather, we played a form of football called "flag" football. This fact, however, meant nothing to my mother who at once flew into a rage. "He is going to get hurt!", she cried. I continued to beg, plead, and explain my burning, inner desire to be a professional athlete. For once, in an unusual twist of events, my father came to my rescue and assured my mother that I would be okay. It seems he wanted me to challenge myself physically. He was, after all, a very strong, athletic man.

I believe it was during the fourth team practice that I proved my mother right. I was playing defense and someone on the other team blocked me for the guy running the ball. I fell. The blocker fell. Then the runner fell. When the runner fell, his knee landed squarely on my left ankle that was held immobile in the pile of kids. The bone in my ankle was broken. This was not an earth shattering disaster. A small cast and six weeks of healing and I was back on the field playing football.

Perhaps you can tell that once upon a time I thought I was going to be an all-star basketball or football player. I was strong, fast, big and tall when I was in sixth grade. But, by the time I made it to high school, I was seriously and indisputably average. I played on the freshman football team at Sam Rayburn High School in Pasadena, Texas because I was still strong and fast. Not surprisingly, the guys around me were also strong and fast. But, I was still good enough to make the starting team where I played both offense and defense.

But, over the summer between my freshman and sophomore years a strange thing happened. It seemed to me that *everyone* around me became *much* larger. As summer came to an end, the football team began two-a-day training. The guys on the team now hit much harder and weighed much more than me. Football practice was becoming quite a painful experience.

One day at the end of training we had a wrestling session. Of course, we were football players and knew next to nothing about wrestling. We simply were paired up and struggled around on the mat, breathing hard and sweating profusely. I was paired up with one of the defensive backs, a strong and mean character named Camacho. I was certain I could hold my own although I also knew the match would cause me more pain.

However, right before my match, the coach tapped me on the shoulder and told me I was to report to the weight room. My friend, Bailey, was going to take my place on the mat. I don't recall the reason for this sudden change of plans.

I do, however, recall the next day. When I reported to the gym for football training, I learned that my friend, Bailey, had broken his neck in the wrestling match. As a result of his injuries he was now in the hospital and was paralyzed. My first though was that this could have (and possibly should have) been me! Yes, I know that all athletic activities have inherent risks. My broken ankle and many other injuries have proven this. But, I can't help but wonder if I might have suffered a similar fate. Bailey and I were almost exactly the same height and build. Not long after this event I decided that not only was I not going to be a superstar football player making millions of bucks, but I was also probably going to end up with a serious injury either on or off the field. After playing a few games more games I packed up my bags, took my jockstrap and retired from high school football. I can't say that I ever regretted the decision. I still have knee and neck issues that I attribute to the physical abuse of two years of high school football.

Story 7 – A Girl and a Shoulder (c. 1973)

I was very busy during my high school years. I studied hard, played in a rock band, acted in school plays and much more. I did not devote very much time to the pursuit of high school girls, but let me make it clear – nothing is more important to high school boys than high school girls.

I was very involved in the Alvin High School a capella choir. I wrote music for the choir and directed a couple of musicals. One of the girls in the choir was named Jennifer. I thought she was cute. We liked each other and spent much time talking. Of course, I believed that the way to "get lucky" with Jennifer was to spend even more time talking with her.

I lived in Manvel, Texas and she lived at home with her parents in Seabrook, Texas. These places were about thirty minutes apart.

One night, I went to her house. We talked and talked. Then, we talked even more. My hormones were in overdrive and making progress with a girl was very important! I left Jennifer's house around midnight and began the drive home. Trying to be witty, intelligent, funny, sexy and clever is apparently quite draining because I dozed off while driving home.

I awoke to the rumbling noise that is generated when a car is driving on the shoulder of the road. I opened my eyes and was disoriented. I was driving about seventy miles per hour and I was on the shoulder of the road. However, the road was on the right side of me! To make matters worse, there was a car approaching at high speed and it was very close.

Operating solely on instinct, I did nothing. I had a big desire to turn the steering wheel hard to the right and quickly return to the lane I was supposed to be in. But, it is a good thing I didn't do this. The approaching car was too close and sped by me on the right. I was on the shoulder and he was in his lane. But, what if he had swerved to the right to avoid the headlights coming at him?

There were so many vividly imagined scenarios in which I ended up in a horrendous, life ending head-on collision. I knew that I had been careless and had once again escaped with no consequences – not even a scratch on the car. I also wondered at what point in my life would someone else do this same thing to me. It was certainly possible that I would be driving along at night and an oncoming driver would fall asleep and drift across the center line toward me. When he awoke, which way would he swerve? Would I be so lucky again?

Story 8 – Magic Bed (c. 1974)

This is the story of the magic bed. When I was a toddler, my uncle Joe lived with my grandmother. There was a driveway that went down the side of the house and continued to a garage in the back of her small house on Glover Street in Houston, Texas. The garage was about 15 steps away from the back of the house and it had a small room attached to it. This is the room in which uncle Joe lived. My grandmother's name was Bertha and Joe was her second son.

In the small room was a bed with a carved wooden headboard. One night, Joe, who liked to drink, fell asleep with a cigarette and caught the bed and much of the small room on fire. The bed, Joe and the garage somehow miraculously survived the incident. I barely knew my uncle Joe who died from lymphoma when I was still a young boy. So, the bed apparently had its first trial by fire in the mid 60's.

My family moved to Manvel, Texas when I was sophomore in high school. During my junior and senior years I was obsessively driven to be successful. There was no limit to my motivation to work harder and harder. I went to school early to study piano and harp, stayed after school to participate in numerous clubs and school plays, and worked late into the night writing music. Many nights I had rehearsals with my band, Obsidian.

I never slept more than about four hours per night. As you might imagine, all of this work and lack of sleep combined to take a toll. I was frequently a tired or sick guy.

By the time I was a senior in high school, I had begun smoking cigarettes. Both of my parents smoked and many of my friends did, too. I know I am making excuses, but it seemed at that time that it was trendy or cool to smoke.

One night I came home late from band practice, spent some time writing music and then went to bed.

Some hours later, I awoke and found that it was difficult to breath. I sat up in bed and noticed nothing out of the ordinary. I stood up and turned on the light. I could see nothing! There was a really thick cloud of smoke that filled the bedroom.

My bedroom was part of a separate building that included the garage and there was a window-mounted air conditioner for cooling. I was disoriented and thought that the air conditioner might be on fire.

Since I couldn't see and I couldn't breath, I opened the door to the garage and left the room. After a few minutes in the smoke-free garage, my mind cleared enough to devise a plan. Since I couldn't see anything with the light on, perhaps I might be able to see where the fire was coming from if I turned off the light. I did this and immediately noticed that the mattress on the bed was glowing red.

Apparently, I had fallen asleep and the lit cigarette I was holding started a fire. It was around 3:00 in the morning and I didn't want to wake my parents, so I carried the mattress outside, put it on the ground, and used the water hose to extinguish the smoldering mattress.

It was at this time that I noticed the extent of the damage. More than half of the mattress was gone. There was, in fact, only barely enough of the mattress remaining to provide space for my body. It seemed to me impossible that I hadn't been burned.

Later I learned that most people simply don't wake up under these conditions. Asphyxiation from mattress smoke inhalation is quite common. And, yes this was the very same bed that Joe had tried to burn up nearly 15 years earlier. Joe had been smoking in a small room behind the main house next to a garage. I had been smoking in a small room behind the main house next to a garage. Weird, huh?

Why did I wake up? How could I have been so lucky that the fire spread all the way around my body but didn't burn me?

I resolved never to smoke in bed again. This, of course is a very sound rule to follow. However, most people don't need to come this close to dying before learning this lesson. (Of course, a better choice is to become a non-smoker.)

About 10 years later, my mom was doing laundry. She brought in a load of clothes from the dryer and threw them on my old bed that was still occupying the same room. Somehow, the heat from the clothing caused them to ignite. This seems a bit strange but that is how my mother explained the event to me. This fire took place during the daytime but there was no one in the room. By the time the fire was discovered, the old bed had finally been destroyed by fire. This bed made it through two fires and several decades, but surviving the third blaze was simply asking too much.

Story 9 – Extra Pay (1975)

After graduating from high school, I packed my bags and headed off to college. One of my primary goals was to move out of the house and get away from my controlling parents. So, I headed to Austin, Texas and the University of Texas. It would have been cheaper and more convenient to stay in town and attend the University of Houston. Or, I could have attended Rice University. I had been accepted there and would, in fact, eventually graduate from Rice. But, that is a story for another time.

I had been lucky enough to receive a cash scholarship from Alvin High School that helped finance my first year in academia and girl chasing at The University of Texas. This place is huge with much to do on campus. The first year went by quickly. But, I didn't know how I was to pay for my second year away from home. Clearly, I needed to get a job.

When summer arrived, I found employment at Catalyst Services in Alvin, Texas. This company provided a variety of cleaning and installation services for catalysts used in the petrochemical industries. (A catalyst is a material that helps chemicals transform from one form to another. This is how many plastics are manufactured.)

Near the end of the summer, the company had a short-term, emergency job at the Texaco Refinery in Port Arthur, Texas. Our job was to remove the platinum catalyst from a spherical benzene reactor, clean it, and replace it. This is necessary since, over time, the catalyst pellets crack and break down. This causes dust and small particles to interfere with the flow of material through the catalyst.

We met at the offices of Catalyst Services and headed out on our two-hour ride together for our first day in Port Arthur. When we arrived, we discovered that the fine folk at Texaco had decided to leave the reactor in service. This was not a good plan. This meant that the reactor was still extremely hot and we could not begin our work.

It is very expensive to shut down a portion of a chemical or refining process. So, not only did they run the reactor until we arrived they also wanted us to begin cleaning the catalyst immediately.

To clean the catalyst, we had a series of machines connected by conveyor belts. We put catalyst into one end of the system and it was carried and shaken and filtered as it travelled to the other end. Dust-free, whole pieces of catalyst emerged as a finished product. Or at least that is how it was supposed to work. However, Texaco in their economically-driven rush to complete the work had created a very dangerous situation.

Benzene is highly flammable. The numerous tons of catalyst we were supposed to clean were coated in benzene along with other reagents. We waited around for several hours while our management argued with Texaco management. Eventually we went to work. The reactor would have taken several days to cool down. It was still over 500 degrees Fahrenheit when we unbolted the access flange and began our work.

We discovered, to our dismay, that as the catalyst came out of the reactor onto the conveyor belt it would spontaneously burst into flames. This is REALLY a bad thing to have happening in a hazardous area of a petrochemical plant. So, you might ask if we stopped work. Well, of course not. We brought in numerous hoses that allowed us to blanket the catalyst in pure nitrogen. Nitrogen removes the available oxygen and effectively suppresses any fire. Unfortunately, we were outside and occasionally the wind would blow, forcing air and oxygen into the machinery and causing small fires or mini-explosions.

Did we stop work because of these dangerous conditions? Of course not. We operated like this for a couple of days. Amazingly, no one was injured by the fires or the mini-explosions. It was simply a hot, miserable, dangerous and toxic working environment.

After several days, my supervisor approached me and asked if I wanted to make some extra money. I said, "SURE!" He told me that the sphere was nearly empty and they needed a couple of people for hazardous duty. I remember thinking, "What could be more hazardous than what we have been doing?" He explained that someone must put on a mask with fresh air and go down inside the sphere in order to shovel the last of the catalyst out of the access flange. The reactor had cooled down dramatically over the past several days but it was not cool. It was still well over one hundred degrees Fahrenheit. Yet, I still volunteered.

The hours dragged on as we waited for my hazardous environment breathing apparatus. The equipment arrived about 3 hours before the end of my shift. So, the supervisor informed me that he wasn't going to have us enter the vessel with so little time remaining on our shift. The next shift was going to enter the sphere and a couple of those guys would get the coveted hazardous-duty pay. I went home that night thinking how unlucky I was that I would miss out on a few extra dollars.

When I arrived at the offices of Catalyst Services the next morning I learned that there had been an accident at the Texaco job. Two of my coworkers and friends had volunteered for the hazardous job. One of the guys was inside the vessel shoveling the catalyst and the other was on top of the sphere feeding him the air hose and the electrical cable for the light so he could see what he was doing.

Apparently, the light he was using ruptured and ignited a flash fire inside the sphere. The man in the reactor was killed and the man at the top, with whom I had attended high school, was seriously burned on his arms and face.

I certainly was not saved by the safety regulations at Texaco nor by the concern for employee safety shown by the managers of Catalyst Services. Only a fortunate equipment delay intervened between me and this tragedy. I could have been burned or killed. Frankly, I am surprised that a flash fire in the middle of a hazardous area didn't cause a much more significant disaster.

Story 10 – Gone in Five Seconds (1978)

I had finally purchased a nice new car. It was a white Pontiac Phoenix. My wife, Beverly, and I were just beginning to get on our feet. We had rented a decent apartment that was a significant upgrade from our previous "efficiency" apartment. This apartment even had covered parking for our nice, new vehicle. These were stalls somewhat like long-term parking at the airport. The spaces were narrow and you had to carefully squeeze your car into your assigned spot. Every few spaces there were poles that held up the metal roof over the spaces. But, we were doing well.

I had a good job that paid well. And, I was still pursuing my dream of becoming a rock star. My rock band, Obsidian, had practice four times each week. We were writing original tunes and rehearsing often in the certainty of landing a record contract. Of course, we knew we were very good and our big break and associated fame would happen any day.

Beverly and I had agreed to try to stop smoking cigarettes. In one of my half-hearted efforts to achieve this goal, I began smoking a pipe as a substitute. This path to becoming a non-smoker did not succeed. But, I chewed quite hard on a pipe stem for many months.

One night, I grabbed my guitar and my pipe and headed out of the back door of our apartment on my way to band practice. I jumped into the Pontiac Phoenix and drove to the exit of the apartment's parking lot. I was running late and I was (as I often was) in a big hurry. Suddenly, I remembered that I had forgotten something. I don't recall what it was. But, I know it was small, important and I could retrieve it quickly.

I turned around and drove to the rear of our apartment complex. This is where the back door of our apartment was located as well as our nearby covered parking spot. I pulled the car right up next to the sidewalk that led to our door. The gear selector in the Phoenix was located on the center console. I shoved the handle into "park", opened the door and ran into the apartment. I didn't even close the car door.

I grabbed what I needed and ran back out. The car was gone!

I couldn't believe that in those few seconds someone could have been standing so close that they could have jumped into our new car and taken it. I ran back in and breathlessly told Beverly what had happened. She followed me outside as I recounted my tale.

That's when I noticed our car. It was at the other end of the parking lot perhaps 30 yards away. The lights were still on and the driver's door was still open.

Suddenly, I became aware of a new problem. The parking lot was full of cars. Surely, my vehicle had collided with another car. How much damage had been done? How many cars had mine hit?

My pipe had fallen into the track where the gear shifter moves. When I had shoved it forward into "park" it hadn't made it all the way. I had accidentally put the car into reverse before I had jumped out and run into the apartment.

The Pontiac had apparently backed up slowly for about thirty yards in a straight line and had then decided to make a sharp turn. It backed up between two parked cars and struck one of the poles holding up the garage roof. It seems the vehicle had been moving quite slowly. There was no visible damage to the car. The corner of the bumper had hit the pole and hadn't even bent it.

My car was found! There was no damage. I hopped into the beautiful new car and headed to band practice.

I was careless and yet there was no penalty. Was this just luck?

Story 11 – Did Alice Do This? (1981)

I had returned to study at Rice University when I was 25 years old. But, I had unfortunately set some rather unrealistic goals for myself when I began the first semester. I was trying to work full time and take 21 semester hours. I really don't know what made me think that I (or anyone else) could handle this amount of work.

It turned out the biggest problem was my computer-programming course. In 1981, computers were becoming commonplace but the field was still in its infancy. For my first computer course, we wrote programs in a language called "FORTRAN". The programs we wrote were typed onto 80-column punch cards and then fed into a computer card reader. If any errors were found, even a minor spelling or syntactic error, the program would fail to run (or crash). This would generate a printout in the back room. After about 10 minutes, I could retrieve the printout and review it to find the error. Only then could I create one or more new punch cards and repeat the process.

80-column Computer Punch Cards

Had I been the only person in the undergraduate computer program or in the computer room this would have still been a slow, tedious process. But, in 1981, computer science was one of the hottest fields of education. It seemed everyone wanted to jump onto the computer bandwagon. As a result, there were often nearly a hundred students trying to use the computer equipment. We were crammed into a stuffy room in the basement. There were long lines to punch the cards. Then you were required to put your cards into a queue for processing. Then you had to wait until the program had been run by the computer technicians and had generated the coveted printout. As a result, I was spending many sleepless nights hanging out in the computer room.

One day, Alice Cooper, a rock band, came to town. After school, I took my girlfriend, Meredith, to see the act. I had not slept in two full days since I knew I needed to finish my programming work before I took one night off to have some fun.

The concert was very good and we had an excellent time. Alice put on a great show with a giant screen above the stage and outrageous theatrics. After the show, we came home and went to bed around midnight. After all, I was exhausted.

When I awoke the following morning I immediately knew that something was terribly wrong. Meredith asked me what was wrong and I told her that I was certain I was dying. There was an incredible pain that felt like I had broken my back. I had no idea what was going on but I knew that it was very bad.

She asked what I wanted to do. I told her that I was going to lie in bed for a little while and see what happened. The intense pain did not change over time and I decided we needed to go to the hospital.

At the time I lived in a third floor apartment on the west side of town. The only hospital with which I was familiar was located near my sister's house in Pasadena on the other side of town.

We slowly walked down the stairs, got into the car, and I drove us to the hospital. Well, I had to do this. Meredith didn't have a driver's license and I didn't want to call for an ambulance. We parked at the hospital near the emergency room and I slowly walked in. Once inside,

I told Meredith that I absolutely could go no further. She went and found someone to help me. They put me in a wheelchair and did a quick examination.

They took a chest x-ray and showed it to me. I could clearly see that I had only one lung! It seems that I had developed a collapsed lung and the pressure inside my chest was preventing the left lung from inflating. The doctor immediately put me on a gurney and inserted a chest tube while I was fully conscious. This was an amazing experience that I would not want to share with anyone else. I want to spare you the horrendous details but I assure you it was very unpleasant. Meredith was attending Texas Women's University and was studying to be an occupational therapist. In this field they work with all types of serious, traumatic job-related injuries. Watching the doctors deal with my situation caused Meredith, who was not squeamish, to pass out.

I asked the doctor what would have happened if I hadn't come to the hospital. He said flatly that I would have died. With the lung in this collapsed state the heart is free to fall over to the side and twist up the coronary arteries.

I spent a week in the hospital. Then I dropped one of my courses. My teachers were very helpful and allowed me to continue coursework from home.

A few weeks later I went for a follow-up visit with my doctor. He told me that this type of collapsed lung usually happens to men between the ages of 18 and 25. (I almost missed it since I was 25 years old at the time.) He also informed me that in about 50% of the cases, the collapsed lung would recur within one year. So, I spent the next year looking over my shoulder. Any pain in my chest or back would indicate to me that this was the big one and once again I was on my way to the emergency room. But, it never happened.

I asked the doctor what I did to cause this. He said that I didn't do anything. But, I often wondered if going without sleep for days at a time contributed to this life-threatening event. What I knew for certain was that my life could change overnight. We have no guarantee of tomorrow and should therefore make the most of each day.

Story 12 – It is a Classic (1982)

As my years at Rice University continued I was forced to reduce the number of hours I worked. When this happened I lost the use of my company supplied vehicle. My sister loaned me some money so I could purchase a 1967 Ford Mustang. It was not in terrible condition but was obviously a mature vehicle. I thought that I might eventually fix up the car since it was a classic. Perhaps I could even make some money on it.

However, once I began using it to travel to and from school, I began to find all of the serious and hidden problems. For example, I discovered that the vent on the hood that provided fresh air for the interior of the vehicle had rusted out internally. This meant that rain would enter the heater and leak onto the floorboard.

In addition to this problem, this car had one of the earliest air conditioning units. Of course, air conditioning is required in the hot and humid weather of Houston, Texas. The air conditioner worked as designed but unfortunately, the radiator was inadequately sized for the heat of the engine and the demands of this new air conditioner feature while operating in the Gulf Coast's hot summers. Overheating was common.

One weekend, I took my girlfriend, Michelle on a trip to San Antonio. During the trip, the engine temperature began to rise. I turned off the air conditioner and stopped at a gas station to check the coolant in the radiator.

I left the engine running so that the coolant would continue to circulate. I put water on the outside of the radiator for several minutes to cool things off and then slowly released the pressure from the radiator cap. These are standard procedures for safely adding water to an overheated engine.

Again, I waited. Everything seemed okay. So, I removed the cap to add some water and coolant. I waited a bit longer – just to be sure.

As I began to add coolant a fountain of superheated antifreeze shot out of the radiator. I was able to move my face out of the way but one of my forearms was covered. The pain was incredible. It seems that the coolant level had become very low and was not circulating as well as I had thought.

Eventually, I was able to replace the coolant and we were on our way to San Antonio. But the burn on my arm was rather severe. Radiator coolant has an oily consistency. It sticks to you when it gets on you. I was buying and applying every cream and ointment I could find. But, it still hurt like hell.

As you can probably tell, I was well aware of the dangers of a vehicle cooling system, I was very concerned about the dangers and I thought I had taken all of the right precautions to prevent this disaster. But, what if the coolant had sprayed into my face and eyes?

Of course, we will never know. But, it seems to me that this was mere inches and milliseconds from something much worse than a painful burn on the arm.

Story 13 – Misfire (c. 1983)

I worked for many years at J T Thorpe. This was an engineering and design company with offices in California and Texas. The division in which I was employed designed, built and serviced furnaces for steel forging and heat-treating. These were generally natural gas-fired furnaces that heated steel to temperatures between 1500 and 2400 degrees Fahrenheit. I worked in all aspects of this business from design to fabrication to service.

One day, I was sent to adjust the gas burners on a furnace located at Proler Steel Corporation in Houston, Texas. Proler was primarily a steel recycling company that bought old cars and scrap metal. They chopped up the old steel (in a machine called the "Prolerizer") and made small ingots to be melted down and reused.

(It is an interesting aside that a couple of decades before this, my mother had worked as a personal secretary for the founder of this company, Jaime Proler.)

Proler Steel was having trouble with one of their furnaces. This particular furnace had two gas-fired burners and one of them wasn't working properly. I didn't know if it was a problem with the air-to-gas ratio, the ignition system or the flame detection system. But, this was my job: figure out what the problem was and fix it.

This furnace was located on a tower about fifty feet off of the ground. Immediately adjacent to the furnace was a control room. There was a walkway that went from the control room to the furnace and then circled around it. Between the walkway and the ground below was nothing but air. Sharp, jagged scrap metal covered the entire area on the ground beneath the walkway, control room and furnace. It looked like something from a futuristic movie.

The burners on this industrial furnace are similar to those in a home gas heating system except they are much bigger. They combine air with natural gas to create a flammable mixture. Then the mixture is ignited with a spark. Once a burner is lit, it will continue to provide a flame until the fuel/air mixture is turned off. There is also a flame monitoring system that will turn off the gas automatically if the flame goes out for any reason.

I first decided to check the spark plug and ignition system. One of the Proler Steel employees came up on the platform to help me. I told him I was going to disconnect the spark plug wire and remove the spark plug. Then we would test it to see if it was generating a spark. I told him to go into the nearby control room and make sure that no one pressed the "ignition" button while I was disconnecting and removing the spark plug.

The burner was elevated a few feet off the platform so that I had to climb up on some piping in order to work on it. I had just pulled the spark plug wire off of the spark plug when, you guessed it, someone in the control room pressed the "ignition" button. I had the spark plug wire in one hand and my other hand was being used to hang on to the burner.

Right here in my life, I have a few seconds missing from my memory. One moment I was hanging on the burner and the next I was several feet away bent over the railing. The jolt had thrown me from the elevated position where the burner was located toward the abyss and certain death on the scrap metal far below. The only thing that saved me was the railing. And, I almost went over the top of the rail. A little bit higher and I would have gone over.

Once I stopped shaking from the electrical shock and the near-death experience, I went back to work and finished repairing the burner. Of course, I had several choice words to share with the Proler employee in the loudest voice I could generate.

Industrial accidents are certainly common. Fortunately for me, my life continued on after this encounter with high-energy electrons and a nearly 5-story drop onto scrap iron.

Story 14 – Abandon Ship (c. 1983)

For a while, I lived with a friend of mine in an apartment complex. I was attending college and Kenny was working for an electrical distributor.

Kenny had purchased an eighteen-foot catamaran. Kenny's Hobie Cat was a lightweight sailboat with two pontoons. This boat was very fun to sail. We would take it down to the Texas City dike on weekends and sail for hours.

The object of sailing the twin-hull catamaran was to get the boat and the sails positioned just right in order to maximize the ship's speed. This light boat with its relatively large sails could really go fast. When the boat was moving rapidly through the water the hull would "sing" and the boat would tip over and ride on only one of the pontoons. It was very thrilling.

One weekend, Kenny and I went to the Texas City dike and put the boat into the water. We sail her out, turned her around, and started building up speed. We didn't get it quite right and we turned the catamaran over. Don't worry, this happened all the time. Remember that the boat was really light? With two people in the water, the boat would be turned so that the wind would help right the boat. Both people would climb onto the hull and pull. This would start to lift the sail out of the water. The wind would hit the sail and soon the boat would be upright once again.

However, this time it didn't work. The water near the Texas City dike is quite shallow. This time, when the catamaran had capsized, the mast managed to get stuck into the mud at the bottom of the bay. Kenny and I pulled and pushed and grunted but we couldn't free the ship.

Finally, we gave up and sat on the hull. We tried to flag down one of the many other ships in the area and get help. But, no luck.

Finally, I decided to swim to shore to get help. In hindsight, two things were wrong with this plan. Firstly, I am a mediocre swimmer at best and, no, we didn't have life jackets. Secondly, while the shore appeared to be only a couple hundred yards away, distances are difficult to judge on the water.

Anyway, I jumped into the water and began swimming for shore. I was getting tired and the shore didn't seem to be getting any closer. But, I kept going. Every few minutes, I would stop, tread water, and look for the shore. Of course, I knew I HAD to make it. There were no options.

I was extremely fatigued when disaster struck. I swam into the middle of a school of jellyfish. I was being stung all over my face, arms and chest. Now, I panicked and was soon unable to control my breathing. So, this is what it felt like to face death. I knew I couldn't go on. And, I couldn't even yell out that I was in trouble.

I clearly remember the feeling of helplessness and hopelessness and of giving up. My arms simply were no longer responding to my brain's instructions. I resigned myself to my inevitable fate and slid beneath the water.

Then, a really strange thing happened. I stood up. I was thirty or forty yards from shore, but the water here was only five feet deep. Yes, I had forgotten that the water near the dike was shallow. That was why the catamaran was stuck in the first place!

I had gone from dying and hopeless to safe (and feeling quite stupid) in a matter of seconds. Now, the jellyfish stings seemed like the least of my worries.

As I made my way to the shore, Kenny passed me on the catamaran. Someone in a speedboat had stopped and helped him right the ship.

Perhaps a little patience would have been a better plan. Or, maybe we should have taken a couple of life vests with us on the catamaran.

I am certainly glad that the water wasn't very deep where I decided to give up.

Story 15 – A Wrench in the Works (c. 1984)

One of the last jobs I worked on for J T Thorpe was on a forge furnace located at the Cameron Iron Works facility near Sealy, Texas. Cameron Iron Works had been the largest client for our division of J T Thorpe for many years. However, the steel industry was changing and Cameron was in trouble. Over the next few years, Cameron Iron Works would close down most of their heat-treating and forging operations in America.

But, on this day, the furnaces were still running.

In addition to complete furnaces, JT Thorpe also sold accessory products. One such product was a pressure controller, called an Epic Controller. Here is the basic principle behind this controller. Furnaces have burners that provide heat. Air and gas are mixed and ignited. The result is flame shooting from many burners to heat the furnace and the metal inside. In the case of a forge furnace, the temperature is usually around 2400 degrees Fahrenheit. This doesn't melt the steel but makes it soft enough (or plastic enough) for forging.

The burning air and gas mixture entering the furnace tends to create a positive pressure inside. If left unchecked, this would result in 2400 degree gas leaking out from every small hole in the furnace walls, doors, and floor. This extremely high temperature gas would damage the furnace. So, high positive pressure is undesirable.

But, on every furnace there is a stack. This stack is used to exhaust the burned gases into the atmosphere. Just like a home chimney, the stack creates a negative pressure and tends to suck the gases out of the furnace. This sucking effect is called fluing.

If left unchecked, a large stack can create a significant negative pressure (or vacuum) on the furnace. This will cause the cool, ambient (or room temperature) air to be pulled into all the small holes in the walls, doors, and floor of the furnace. This causes the furnace interior to cool down and requires additional fuel to heat the metal. It can also cause nonuniform temperature spots inside the furnace wherever the cold air is being sucked in.

To solve both of these problems, a sensor is used to measure the pressure in the furnace. A damper is placed inside to the stack in order to control the fluing effect. The pressure controller adjusts the damper so that there is always a very slight positive pressure inside the furnace.

Cameron Iron Works was having problems with this pressure controller. My job was to calibrate the unit.

Here is the problem.

On this particular furnace, someone (in their infinite wisdom) had mounted the pressure controller inside the large control cabinet with all of the other equipment. This cabinet was about six feet wide, eight feet tall, and three feet deep. It was big enough so that a person could stand inside it. However, there was a lot of equipment in this cabinet and all of it was powered. Cameron would not allow me to shut down the furnace in order to calibrate the pressure controller.

I arrived at the site and began working on the Epic pressure controller. I was unable to attach my pressure and electrical equipment to the controller while I knelt outside of the cabinet. So, I carefully climbed into the cabinet. I was using a 12" crescent wrench to disconnect the pressure piping to the Epic controller when my elbow inadvertently made contact with something. That something was a 440-volt motor starter. A large blower was used to push air into the many burners on the furnace. On this blower was a large motor that required much energy so it was connected to a 440-volt power source.

If you have ever been shocked by 120 volts, then you know it is unpleasant. Even more unpleasant is the feeling that 240 volts gives you when those little electrons do their thing. But, 440 volts is not really like a painful feeling. It is more like being hit by a linebacker.

When my elbow made contact with the motor starter my body convulsed and I had the wind knocked out of me. Fortunately, I didn't fall in the cabinet and get electrocuted on some other live circuit.

As I crawled out of the cabinet I realized that I didn't have my crescent wrench. The furnace I was working on was located in a huge building. Lying on the concrete about 50 yards way was my crescent wrench.

I went over and retrieved it. Missing was one-half inch of the metal on the end of the wrench. It had burned off from the current. I had a small burn on my elbow but nothing more.

And, guess what? I had to crawl back inside the cabinet to finish my job. Now I was even more careful if such a thing were possible.

The takeaway here is that it is unwise to agree to work on electrical equipment while it is powered. This is especially true for 440-volt equipment.

Story 16 - On the Runway (c. 1986)

After finally graduating from college and joining the workforce, I decided that I would take a vacation. After all, I had never really had one before. I was single and I could go anywhere. I chose a Club Med vacation resort for singles. The resort was on the Pacific side of Mexico in a town called Ixtapa. It was winter in Houston so I was especially excited about a week in the warm sun with beautiful beaches and lots of single ladies. I planned to return to work with a nice tan and make everyone jealous.

The week there was indeed very nice. The food, people, and activities were very enjoyable. Fresh mango and papaya were served with every meal. It was hot, sunny and clear each day. I played in the sand on the rock-strewn beaches, floated in the pool and flirted with many pretty ladies. Unfortunately, my week in paradise came to an end much too soon.

So, I packed up all my belonging and headed to the airport for what should have been a short flight back to Houston. The flight was due to depart rather late in the day and my brother-in-law had previously agreed to pick me up at the Houston Intercontinental airport upon my arrival. The flight back was scheduled to make one quick stop in a small city called Zihuateneho. It was in this city where my adventure really begins.

At this point in my life I was 30 years old and I felt there was absolutely no need for me to speak Spanish. My ex-wife had been raised in Spain and had tried to interest me in studying the language for several years. I had studied French in college and I had never needed *that* language so I was certain that I wouldn't need to study Spanish either. Everywhere I went English was spoken. This had been true for the entirety of my vacation to Ixtapa. There were no language problems.

When we made our stop in Zihuateneho, the flight attendant announced that we should exit the plane in order to go through customs. Hmmm. I had never traveled outside the country and I didn't really know what that meant. They told us we could leave everything on the plane but I didn't trust this suggestion. I had an Olympus camera with several expensive lenses and a tripod in a camera bag. I protectively grabbed my bag of expensive gear as I exited the plane.

As I descended the stairs from the plane onto the runway, I saw there were two busses waiting. A Mexican (who was holding a carbine) pointed to the bus on the right. I asked, "United States"? He replied, "Zihuateneho". I replied and insisted, "I am going to the United States". Once again, he used his carbine to point me toward the bus on the right. I did as I was told. I climbed aboard the indicated bus.

The bus took us to a building and let us off. I entered with a few other passengers and found I was in a small, grimy room with a conveyor belt. The low ceiling and dim fluorescent lighting did not give me a feeling of inner peace. This conveyor belt was bringing luggage from the airplane into the room.

I thought this was odd but perhaps we needed to collect our luggage and then go through customs. Then we would simply board the plane again.

There was another guard posted at the exit from this room. I approached him and asked him if this was the case. Unfortunately, this guard, too, was also unable to speak any English. So, I patiently waited for my luggage to come from outside on the conveyor belt. Luggage came. People left. I soon began to panic. There was no more luggage on the belt and everyone who had been in the room with me had already departed. The guard was unable to help me and he wouldn't allow me to leave the room, so I (in a fit of complete insanity) decided to take matters into my own hands. I knew there were people who spoke English on my plane. If I could only get to them and explain the situation......

I climbed onto the conveyor belt, and crawled out of the building on my hands and knees. Now, I was outside of the building. I could see airplanes sitting on the concrete. One of them had stairs. I slung my camera bag over my shoulder and ran toward the plane. When I arrived, I climbed the stairs and was met by a flight attendant. I asked if this was the flight to Houston. She didn't say I was stupid and I couldn't just climb up to her plane. In fact, she didn't seem overly shocked by my appearance at the top of the stairs to her plane. She simply said "No". This plane was not going to Houston. She, in fact, pointed to another plane and said, "Maybe it is that one."

I climbed down the stairs and began running toward the next plane. That is when I saw *them*.

A jeep was speeding across the concrete toward me. It had a machine gun mounted on it and there were four armed soldiers. They were saying something to me in Spanish through a megaphone.

Until this moment it hadn't occurred to me that a white guy wearing sandals, shorts, and a tank top should not be running across airport runways. This is probably true everywhere. But, I think it is an especially bad idea in Zihuateneho, Mexico. In addition, I had a camera bag across my shoulder with a tripod sticking out of it. At night the tripod could look like a gun. I did the only thing I could think of doing. I froze right where I was and put my hands in the air.

The soldiers stopped their jeep near me. They were all holding their carbines but fortunately were not pointing them at my head. They motioned for me to get into the jeep and I followed their instructions. None of these soldiers spoke English. So, I sat quietly while we drove.

They took me to the airport and put me in some seats near the Aero Mexico office. I sat there for about an hour. Of course I realized that my brother-in-law was not going to be able to pick me up at the airport. This was before the age of cell phones so I could not call him and let him know where I was. I also figured I was in enough trouble that I might not be allowed to make a phone call. After all, I had no idea what the penalty for an escaped American prisoner from a luggage room who was recaptured while chasing parked aircraft across a runway was.

I sat there in the airport. Alone. It was becoming later and later and now there were few people to be seen. Then I heard an announcement over the airport speakers that said, in both Spanish and English, the airport would be closing in 10 minutes. This news did not make me feel better. I was in an airport in a small town in Mexico. I had no money.

Things seemed hopeless. I was beginning to think I should learn some Spanish.

Then a man came out of the Aero Mexico office and approached me. In English, he invited me to come into the office. He motioned for me to sit and I did. He then asked me why I was running across the runway. With increasing anxiety I explained the whole story to him. When I had finished my saga, he said simply, "The men at the buses are supposed to be able to speak English." This guy didn't seem angry. In fact, he actually seemed sympathetic to my plight.

Then he said that there were no more flights to the United States tonight. He said the best he could do was to fly me to Mexico City. Then I could catch an early flight to Houston tomorrow morning. I told him that I had no money. Well, I had 28 pesos. This was at a time when it was 2400 pesos per dollar. So, I had actually a little more than one cent. He assured me that they would take care of everything. He laid out the plan. I would be flown to Mexico City tonight. A driver would take me to a hotel. They would pay for the taxi and the hotel. In the morning the driver would pick me up and take me to the airport where I would then catch a flight to Houston.

I told him about my brother-in-law. He said he would contact the airport in Houston and get in touch with my brother-in-law to let him know I was safe and what our plan was.

This was a great relief! We had a plan. But, after the adrenaline rush I was exhausted. It was also getting late.

Soon, I was on a flight to Mexico City. Unfortunately, Mexico City is in the mountains at an elevation of 4000 feet. It was winter and in Mexico City it was 45 degrees. I had sandals, shorts and a tank top. My luggage was in Houston. So, any time spent outside was quite painful.

I arrived at the hotel around midnight and I was very hungry. As you might imagine the main restaurants were closed. But I found a small place to serve me a sandwich and some coffee. And, strangely enough, I was not alone in the restaurant.

There was a lady from Alaska with her two children also having a late snack. She had come to Mexico to escape Alaska's winter cold and darkness. I struck up a conversation with her and I told her my story. As I recounted my tale, I realized I had two additional problems. It was now 1:00 in the morning and I needed to wake up at 4:00 for my ride back to the airport. How was I going to wake up after 3 hours of sleep?

This lady, whom I had just met, offered to loan me her alarm clock.

I told her that I also wore contacts. In those days, I wore hard contact lenses. These should be removed every night and cleaned. I had no contact lens cleaning solution, my contacts had been in for a very long time already, and my eyes were feeling very bad.

Once again, she came to my rescue. I followed her to her room where she gave me the clock and contact solution. (I didn't borrow her toothbrush although I really needed one.)

The next morning at 4:30 a.m. I knocked on her door and returned her clock and contact solution with profuse thanks. Then I was taken to the airport and caught my flight back to Houston. My wonderful brother-in-law was waiting at the gate for me. My relaxing Mexican vacation had come to a pleasant conclusion.

Now, it is probably rare that an American is found running across the runways of a Mexican airport late at night. And, I have never heard of any such American being shot while sprinting toward a parked jet. But, for a brief moment there, I thought I could have been the first victim. In my mind I could hear the .500 caliber machine gun rounds approaching me from behind…

I should make it clear that I no longer crawl out of airport baggage claim areas via the conveyor belt. However, there is no doubt that this behavior gave the airport employees something to talk about for many months. *"Remember when that crazy gringo crawled out of the baggage room and went running across the runway?"*

Story 17 - Close the Business (c. 1987)

In 1983, I was nearing the completion of my degree at Rice University. I also needed money. College is very expensive and is even more so when you are already an adult. I had an apartment, a car and credit card bills. So, I started a business as a sideline in 1983 in order to help supplement my income from J T Thorpe, which had been seriously reduced. By 1986, when I graduated, the business had grown significantly and I decided to incorporate and take on some business partners. This was the "big time". Going from a sole proprietorship to a full-fledged C-Corporation complete with articles and by-laws made me feel like a true grownup. As I had hoped, bringing on two other shareholders caused even further company growth.

The company, Specialty Control Systems, had two basic sources of revenue: 1) software development; and 2) electrical control systems. I had degrees in electrical engineering and computer science. I was the only technical employee we had. Bob sold my software skills and Kenny sold electrical equipment and my engineering and design skills.

Eventually, I had to quit my high paying job at Intermetrics and go to work full-time for Specialty Control Systems. In the beginning, things were good. We had a contract to develop a tank level monitoring system (software) and we had numerous state highway control systems to manufacture.

However, all businesses have their ups and downs. In my case, most of the "downs" had to do with my business partners. After a few contracts for tank level monitoring systems, Bob decided that he didn't want to do sales work. He wanted to develop pre-packaged software and market this nationally. To do this, he wanted to borrow $1 million and spend it on development and marketing. Personally, I hate debt. And, I didn't think the plan would work. But, since Bob was not selling software systems we had no revenue from this side of the business.

Kenny, on the other hand, was having marital problems. His wife was trying to take all of his assets in a viciously disputed divorce. As a result, Kenny simply didn't want to generate any more assets that his soon-to-be ex-wife might acquire.

These circumstances conspired to reduce my income to virtually zero. I had a new corporation and we had bills such as rent and electricity. I also had a wife who had a habit of spending money. In short, I was in deep trouble.

I could close the company and go find a job. There was still a high demand for people with my skill set. But, I was committed to making this new business successful.

I explained my dedication to making the company a success and the company's current dire situation to my wife, Cindy. She had a good job and assured me that she would support my decision.

I contacted a temporary employment agency. I am an excellent typist, so I took on part-time jobs typing. Most of this work was for Lockheed, a NASA contractor.

But, things were not improving. Bob refused to make sales calls. We had expenses but no revenues to cover them.

Just as things seemed they couldn't get worse and I was almost ready to give up on this entrepreneurial dream, I received the call that changed everything. My sister, Linda, called to tell me she wanted to talk to me about developing new software for her company, Wolfenson Electric. She worked there in the position of Secretary/Treasurer and Comptroller.

I had been providing support for their aging TI-990 minicomputer for many years. Recently, Texas Instruments had informed her that the TI-990 system would no longer be supported and their accounting software could not be transferred to the newer model. This angered her and made her disillusioned with Texas Instruments. The software they used had been heavily customized for Wolfenson Electric's need. Now, they had a big problem. Therefore, she contacted me.

She asked me if I was interested in developing a complete accounting package for Wolfenson Electric. I told her that I could write any kind of software package but that I knew very little about accounting systems. She assured me that she would teach me everything I needed to know.

So, just like that, Specialty Control Systems went from the verge of bankruptcy to profitability. For the next five years, we sold personal computers, networking equipment, and software to Wolfenson Electric. The accounting software that we developed for them is still being used by Specialty Control Systems for our accounting needs. Also, as a result of the development work we did for Wolfenson Electric, we acquired new skills in computer networking and in accounting software systems. We were able to use these new selling points to acquire additional customers.

I really don't know what would have happened if my sister had not called when she did. I probably would have been required to seek other employment and my fledgling company would have been forced to close.

Story 18 - Road Rally (c. 1988)

In 1988, my wife, Cindy, worked as branch manager for Kelly Services, one of the largest temporary employment agencies in America. Kelly Services frequently held events to build employee loyalty and camaraderie. On one spring weekend, they held such an event.

This time it was a "road rally". The way this road rally worked was as follows. Each employee and their spouse were given a list of locations and questions. The objective was to drive around Houston to each of these locations and discover the answer to the questions. Cindy and I found the activity to be fun and entertaining.

To help the entertainment value, we each had a mixed drink that we sipped as we navigated our road rally challenge. Our choice of beverage at that time was Crown and 7-up. We probably had more than one. We were having a good time.

Following the instructions to each new destination was challenging. This was prior to the advent of Google Maps and built-in navigation. In other words, everyone had to read a map in order to make there way around the complex back streets of downtown Houston.

Cindy and I were talking, drinking and trying to read a map when suddenly she yelled, "Look Out!". There, crossing the street in front of us, was a very young, black child. She was crossing the street at an intersection. She was alone. There was no stop sign, crosswalk, or traffic light.

I slammed on the brakes and was barely able to avoid running over the girl, who was probably only 6 or 7 years old.

I am certain that the penalties would have been high if a white guy ran over a small, black child while he and his wife were drinking Crown and Seven-Up. Even without civil or criminal penalties I would have been devastated.

But, I was lucky. I have no DWI or DUI incidents on my driving or criminal history. I had no manslaughter charges to explain to prospective employers.

I wasn't drunk. I wasn't even violating any traffic laws. However, none of this would have mattered. I was just seconds away and feet away from a life-altering event. I could have been standing in front of a judge pleading my case. How differently could my life have turned out?

Story 19 - Change Lanes (c. 1989)

I am sure that every driver has a long list of highway related near misses. There are many accidents and traffic deaths each year. But, this is a collection of stories about what could have been. So, please bear with me for one more, near-tragic automobile story.

I was driving a sports car, a Nissan 300 ZX, and was returning to the office from a sales call. I was heading southbound on interstate 45 just south of loop 610 in Houston.

As anyone who has lived in Houston for a while can tell you, IH 45 has ALWAYS been under construction. I have lived in Houston my entire life. The only question one might ask is what part of IH 45 is under construction today. As soon as they finish one part, they begin construction on another part. And, associated with this construction are traffic cones, merging lanes, confusing signs, heavy machinery and other items that encourage accidents.

I was driving in the left lane, the fast lane, and I was just about to pass a very large dump truck. I noticed as I approached the big truck that he was moving into my lane. So, I slowly started moving toward the left and onto the shoulder of the road.

My attention was on the big truck and its huge tires. The Nissan was a very low profile vehicle. In a battle between our two machines, there was no question which one of us would win.

Suddenly, the truck started coming completely and rapidly into my lane. I swerved into the shoulder lane.

That was when my life passed in front of my eyes. I was traveling at least 70 miles per hour and without warning the shoulder lane ended. Not only did it end, but some construction idiot had set one of those concrete freeway dividers in the dead center of the shoulder lane. These are the barriers that keep one direction of traffic from crossing over to the other side. They are smooth and curved and are designed so that cars can run into them with minimum damage. These were about twenty feet long and about four feet high. However, I was racing directly at the butt end of one of these. There were no barrels to absorb even a small amount of the destructive energy of the impact.

There was absolutely no way I could not stop and in a couple of seconds I was destined to run head-on into the edge of a four-foot high concrete barrier. This was going to be very bad. And, cars in those days did not have air bags.

Something in my driving experience told me it was better to hit an object that was moving in the same direction I was than to smash into a stationary object or an object going the opposite direction. So, without hesitation I swerved hard to the right knowing that I would be crushed under the wheels of the dump truck. My other choice was simply much worse.

Concrete Freeway Dividers

Then a miracle occurred. The truck swerved hard to the right at exactly the same time I swerved. I was back in my lane and the truck was back in its lane.

My heart was pounding. What had just happened?

I slowed down and let the truck move ahead of me. These were the years when cell phones had first made an appearance. There was a sign on the back of the dump truck that read, "How's my driving?" I dialed the number.

A lady answered the phone immediately. I began to explain that I had almost been killed by one of their trucks. She said that she had the driver on the other line. The driver had swerved because another car had pulled in front of him. He had seen the misplaced concrete barrier and had also swerved back just in time. The lady and the driver were both very apologetic. There was nothing more to say. There was no damage and no one had been injured. I just ended the call.

In the end, it was just another exciting day of driving through the construction zones on interstate 45 in Houston. But, there is a lesson here. While driving one should always look far ahead and plan for some unusual driving behavior from those nearby.

Story 20 – Mountain Surprise (1999)

One of my favorite pastimes is to go hiking in the mountains. Each day we are pummeled with a barrage of noises and images from televisions, smart phones, social media, billboards, politicians, airplanes flying above us, and much more. We breathe the canned atmosphere inside air-conditioned buildings. Much of our days are spent sitting at a desk, watching television, or riding in a vehicle.

At a deep level, my eyes, ears, sense of smell, and my muscles all yearn to be outside, climbing, absorbing the sights and sounds of nature. The nearby Rocky Mountains are beautiful in every season. And, far away from the bustle of city life, the only sounds that are heard are the rush of water in one of the clear streams splashing off of boulders or the rustling of gentle breezes through the aspen and pine trees. The silence there can be deafening.

When I first decided that I wanted to take up solo hiking in the mountains, I approached the project slowly and methodically. I did research. I purchased all the equipment I had read would be necessary: tent, stove, water filtering equipment, food, boots, sleeping bag and much more. I made a two-column, concise list with check boxes. (I am an engineer after all.) I went on an overnight hike in order to test the equipment. My test hike was in Texas where I quickly discovered it is much hotter than in the mountains. I was sweating profusely and quickly used up all of the water I had packed. I did find a nearly dried up stream however and was able to filter more water so that I didn't die of thirst.

At the completion of my test hike I thought I was ready to head for the mountains. I have relatives near Denver, Colorado and I have been into Rocky Mountain National Park near Estes Park, Colorado on many occasions going all the way back to my childhood. This, however, was going to be my first solo overnight hike into the mountains. I preferred to avoid the crowds so I planned my trip in early September after Labor

Day when the kids had returned to school. After all the point of hiking is quiet and solitude.

When I arrived in Denver, I met with some of my relatives and we had a nice breakfast. Then I headed into the mountains. The first day of hiking was planned to be a day hike. I would climb up and down during the day to help my body become acclimatized to the altitude. I would be climbing to around 10,000 feet and the air is quite thin for someone who lives in Houston, Texas near sea level.

The day hike went well. The weight of the pack felt good and I was excited to spend my first night alone in the mountains.

The campsite I had reserved was near Fern Lake and was about 7 miles from the trailhead. The air was crisp and the scenery was breathtaking. I took my time on the hike. I didn't have a deadline other than setting up camp before nightfall. The campsite was located about 100 yards from a mountain stream and away from the rarely traveled trail. Most day hikers do not travel this far into the mountains. Destinations like this one were mostly visited by overnight, serious hikers.

I set up camp and cooked some dinner. Food tastes delicious after you have carried a heavy pack for many hours. I hung up the remaining food (to discourage bears) and enjoyed the setting sun. As the temperature began to fall, I crawled into the tent and tried to sleep.

It is difficult for me to sleep in strange places under the best of conditions. However, it was quite cold and there were numerous unusual noises. As I lay there in the dark the hours crept by slowly.

Sometime in the middle of the night I suddenly heard something that sounded like the heavy exhalation of a bear. (Yes, I know I have an overactive imagination.) I lay there and waited. About 30 minutes later I heard it again. Finally, I mustered the courage to open the tent and look outside. (The worst thing that could happen would be hand to hand combat with a black bear.)

When I opened the tent, a pile of snow slid off the tent and down the back of my neck. This is what the sound was. As snow built up on the tent, eventually it would become too heavy and would slide. The sliding piles of snow sounded like a heavy exhalation. I scraped the snow off the tent and climbed back inside.

Then I really began to worry. I was completely unprepared for snow!

As soon as the sun came up I exited the tent in a panicked state. It was snowing heavily and everywhere I looked was a thick blanket of white. Everything I had left lying on the ground was buried beneath six inches of snow or more. I managed to make some coffee, locate my equipment and pack up my tent. This was difficult because I was trying to roll and fold up a tent and sleeping back while it was snowing heavily. Once everything was back in the pack I looked around and realized that I had no idea where the trail was. It was difficult to follow the trail sometimes without snow. Now, I was certain that if I could find where the trail started I would be unable to follow it out of the mountains. My heart was pounding.

Tent in Snow – Rocky Mountain National Park 1999

Hiking out of my lovely mountain retreat was difficult since each step sunk 12 inches into the snow. I couldn't see the loose rocks and uneven terrain under the snow. Often, on one edge of the trail was a steep dropoff. I tried to insure that if I slipped and fell with my heavy pack I would fall TOWARD the mountain. I walked faster.

I noticed paw prints on the trail in the fresh snow. It looked like mountain lion paws. I didn't see the mountain lion. But, I walked even faster.

After about an hour I stopped to drink some water. The water bottle I had inside my coat was frozen solid. The temperature was about 20 degrees Fahrenheit. The snowflakes were huge and were falling so fast that it was difficult to breathe. I walked faster.

I made it back to the trailhead in about 2 hours. This is a rapid pace – even without snow.

Then I noticed the parking lot at the trailhead. There were about 50 large white piles of snow. Hell, I had a rented car. I had no idea what it looked like. I managed to find my car keys and began going from car to car scraping the snow off of the license plates.

Back at the Trailhead – Rocky Mountain National Park 1999

Once I found my car and had unburied it from the snow I began the treacherous drive down the mountain. I had no tire chains and the roads had not been cleared. There were cars on the sides of the road. There were frozen bridges. The adrenaline was still pumping in my bloodstream.

I finally made it off the mountain and back to my hotel room. I took a hot shower and passed out. I was exhausted. By noon, my Colorado relatives were calling me. They said there was a freak, early blizzard that had hit Rocky Mountain National Park last night and they were worried about me.

Yep. I had been worried about me too. But, they say that when you fall off of a bicycle the only sensible thing to do is to get back on the bicycle.

Story 21 – Big Toe (c. 2002)

I have been fortunate to have lived during a wonderful age of almost limitless technological advances. We have moved from slide rules and before that the abacus) to laptop computers and smart phone calculators. I have seen the evolution of in-home entertainment morph from the television that we watched on a huge, heavy black and white unit with a cathode ray tube to streaming our favorite movies today on a high-resolution, wide, LED flat screen with Dolby surround sound.

There have also been numerous amazing medical breakthroughs. One of these is LASIK eye surgery. Using a medical laser, a portion of the eye's lens is burned away and the lens is reshaped to provide improved vision. As a child, I was myopic (or near-sighted). So, I wore glasses in high school and college. In my early 40s I decided to undergo LASIK eye surgery so that I would no longer need glasses.

I went to see the laser-eye-guy for a consultation. He told me, "Certainly!", we can perform LASIK surgery on you (for a nominal fee). He told me that after surgical correction I would be able to see normally at distance. He then told me that, unfortunately due to my advancing age and the associated loss of focal length accommodation, I would probably need to wear reading glasses.

I said, "What?!?" The whole reason I was considering this rather scary eye surgery stuff was to eliminate the need for contacts and glasses. I was competing in Tae Kwon Do tournaments and I was afraid that an impact to my eyes while wearing contacts might cause additional injury. In addition, each morning I woke up and really couldn't see much until I located my ever-elusive glasses.

I expressed my dismay to the laser-eye-surgery-salesman. He said that, if it were his eyes, he would opt for mono-vision LASIK eye surgery. This was (and still is) a procedure where the lens of one eye is partially vaporized in order to allow it to see clearly at a distance and the lens of the other eye is reshaped to see clearly up close. In other words, the vision of the two eyes is purposefully made different.

The eye surgeon told me that after mono-vision surgery I would not need glasses. I could read well, using the "up-close" eye, and I could see clearly at a distance using the other eye. I asked the doctor, "How does the brain know which eye to use?" He told me that it takes time to get used to it but that eventually the brain will ignore the out of focus eye and use only the one with the clear image.

Firstly, I didn't want to wear glasses or contacts. Secondly, I was sure that the doctor knew best. Didn't he? Doctors always have our best interest at heart. They take some kind of oath. So, I signed the contract and handed over my money.

Immediately after the surgery I was very excited. I could see! I could see leaves on trees and I could read. I could do all of this without glasses. I was very pleased.

But, eventually I began to see the disadvantages of mono vision LASIK eye surgery. When I read, I needed to turn my head to the right so that I could use my left (up-close-eye) to scan the page. And, when I looked at something in the distance, I was only able to see it with my right eye. As I soon discovered, these vision limitations compromised my athletic skills.

I went to Dallas, Texas to compete in a Tae Kwon Do tournament. I was fighting another 4th degree black belt. The first round went well and we were tied on points. I had discovered in the first round that the opponent liked to use a roundhouse kick with his right foot. I had a plan to lure him into using this technique, narrowly avoid the kick, and then counterattack. Shortly after the second round began, everything fell into place. I faked a kick with my right foot. He quickly shifted and executed his favorite roundhouse kick. I leaned back to avoid the kick.

Unfortunately, I didn't lean back quite far enough. The big toe of my opponent's right foot hit me in the left eye. This was not good. I could not see out of my left eye. The referee called a time out and stopped the fight. He asked if I was okay. I told him that I was not okay and that I couldn't see out of my left eye. I forfeited the match and went to seek help from the medical people working the tournament.

Within about 15 minutes some of my vision returned. The physician assured me that the impact had missed my cornea and I simply had blunt trauma to the side of my eye. He predicted a full recovery.

About five years earlier I had barely kicked a young lady in the mouth while practicing some fighting techniques. My toenail had split her lower lip and required numerous stitches. I had not kicked her hard and I didn't kick her in the eye.

I was once again very lucky that I hadn't been more seriously injured. If the toenail had hit my cornea the damage might have been serious and permanent. Whenever you get into the ring to fight someone you run the risk of getting hurt. So, I didn't blame the opponent. His job was to try and kick me.

I did however discover one of the drawbacks of mono vision LASIK eye surgery. Since only one eye is working at a time, this mono vision concept completely disables our binocular or stereoscopic vision. Two eyes are required to enable us to clearly perceive distances and create a 3D representation of the world around us.

I had felt that something was wrong whenever I was fighting. Now, I knew what it was. I was unable to accurately judge the distance to my opponent or clearly predict where his foot would land.

Rather quickly I inserted a contact into my "up-close-eye" so that the vision in both my eyes matched. I disabled the mono vision and returned to seeing the world with two eyes.

Yes, sometimes I must now use glasses in order to read fine print, but this is actually quite rare. Being able to see the world through two, uninjured eyes is worth this slight inconvenience. I once again see the world in 3-D and have normal depth perception.

To recap what I do now…. I wear one contact to "undo" the LASIK eye surgery. Now, both eyes have the same acuity. If I am reading small print for long periods of time then I wear glasses on top of my contact. This is rather strange and never fails to amuse my optometrist.

Story 22 - Alternate Route (2002)

I went back into the mountains of Colorado with a new respect for the dangers that are ever present in the wilderness. I decided that there would be less chance of a surprise blizzard if I went hiking in the springtime. I still wanted to avoid the summer crowds so I planned my trip in April before school adjourned for the summer.

This was to be another solo overnight hike. This time I reserved a campsite along a mountain stream that made its way higher and higher up to Sky Pond. As before, I hiked in about seven miles and set up camp. The weather was clear and crisp. It was an unhurried and beautiful trek in the mountains.

I set up my tent, refilled my water bottles and cooked a nice meal. Just at dusk a small red fox came wandering into the campsite. He looked at me and I looked at him. Then he scampered off. I had brought one can of beer and put it into the cold mountain stream. It was a perfect evening in the mountains. My legs were tired from the hike but I felt great. The next day I had planned to hike further up the stream. But this journey would be much easier because I didn't need to carry the heavy pack with the tent and food. I would take a small day-pack and enjoy the streams and lakes at the higher altitudes in the mountains.

And, it started off exactly as planned. I spent some time along a lovely mountain lake where I found a fellow hiker fly-fishing. Everything was peaceful and there was no wind. The water on the lake looked like glass. Then, I followed the trail further upward along the mountain stream. There had been a lot of snow in the mountains during the previous winter. Some of this snow remained at the higher elevations. Soon, I was encountering some deep drifts of snow in which I sank up to my knees. This was not nearly as bad as waking up in a blizzard. Besides, this time I was prepared. I had "gators" on top of my shoes to prevent the snow from entering my boots as I post-holed in the snow. I continued my hike.

Suddenly, the trail I was hiking was completely blocked. There was a wall of snow in front of me that soared to fifteen or twenty feet in height. It was almost vertical. For a short time I thought about scrambling up the pile of snow. However, I knew I would sink into it and I would get very wet. I tested my theory and became convinced that I could not climb over the snowdrift.

Then I noticed a path that veered off the right and seemed to go around the huge pile of snow. I followed it for about for about fifty yards where it suddenly ended. It was gorgeous. The path I was on had ended directly above the stream I was following.

This is when I began to put the pieces of the puzzle together. All trails in the mountains have a steep rise on one side and a drop-off on the other side. If the trail is blocked, the only way to go around will be to go up or go down. I had done neither.

Secondly, there is simply no way that a trail could end suspended twenty feet above a river. I was standing on an ice bridge. And, as I turned to go back I realized that the snow and ice were not really very thick. This was springtime and everything was melting.

Now I also noticed that the bridge was really very slippery and was rounded on the top. It was a great recipe for disaster. If the ice bridge collapsed or I slipped off of it I would fall twenty feet onto the boulders in the river. In addition to the certainty of injury, I would get soaked in the river's water. I was many miles from my camp and any dry clothing. The temperature was in the thirties. So, I was certain to experience hypothermia.

I was tense and afraid as I crawled on my hands and knees back across the ice bridge. When I reached the trail below I could clearly see the danger I had been in. I took a photo so I could remember what I *should have seen* when I was approaching the blocked trail. It seemed strange that I had been unable to recognize the danger as I had calmly walked across the bridge the first time.

Ice Bridge – Rocky Mountain National Park 2002

Oh, well. That disaster hadn't really happened. So, I made my way back to camp while still in a slight state of shock. A momentary lapse of attention and poor judgment had almost turned into a disaster.

Although I love the solitude of the mountains in early spring and in late fall, I now much prefer to go hiking with a friend. There are dangers in the mountains and having someone to watch your back in case of emergency now seems like a very good idea.

Story 23 - Merry Christmas (2003)

My wife, Alexandra, was born in Moscow, Russia. Shortly after I met her, I decided that I wanted to know something about the Russian language and the Russian culture. Not only was I curious about this far off land but I also felt it would help me understand Alexandra better and it would draw us closer.

There are a wide variety of cultures in the United States. People in New York are quite different from those in Houston, New Orleans, or San Diego. The cultural gap between countries is even larger. I had already been exposed to the cultures of Germany (through my grandparents), Mexico (because I live in Houston), and Korea (since I had studied Tae Kwon Do for 30 years). Now, I was intent to lower my ignorance about Russia. I had been fed propaganda about this country (formerly the Soviet Union) when I was a child. During those cold war years the government painted a picture of Russia that included poor peasants and their evil communist government. I wondered what this huge country was really like.

In order to find out about Russian people, the Kremlin, the Bolshoi Theater, dancing bears and nesting dolls I arranged my first trip to visit Moscow shortly after I met Alexandra. It was Christmastime and I would be staying in an upscale, downtown hotel called Hotel National. It was very close to the Kremlin and other important government offices in the heart of Moscow. Fortunately for me, one of Alexandra's friends, Larissa, spoke some English and had volunteered to assist me during my visit.

Unlike many places I have visited across the globe, when I went to visit Moscow there were few people there who spoke English. Signs and menus were printed in Cyrillic. If you didn't understand the Russian language everything would be quite difficult. I had booked several excursions to see museums, churches and nearby cities. Larissa had coordinated a tour guide to help show me around. The guide spoke English very well and had a slightly British accent.

Hotel National – Moscow, Russia (Near Red Square)

Each morning during my stay, I would awaken, have some coffee, and step outside of the hotel. There, at around 8:00 a.m., the same doorman greeted me each day. He stood in the cold air next to a Christmas tree as he waited to open the door for hotel guests. Chatting as best I could with the doorman, I waited for my tour guide each morning.

I saw more churches and museums than I ever want to see again. They were beautiful and interesting, but four days of this activity was way too much. I found out later that Alexandra had purposely tried to keep me busy with these types of activities so that I wouldn't run into other Russian women. Russian women are incredibly beautiful and at that time, many were looking for American men in order to emigrate. The Russian economy was not great and there was more opportunity in America. Plus, there were many more Russian women than there were Russian men.

Alexandra's strategy was successful. I didn't find myself in any social situations with young, beautiful Russian women. I did, however, see plenty of them. And, yes they were indeed very pretty. Each day, when my tour guide dropped me off at Hotel National, I would wander around the downtown area on foot. About one hundred yards around the corner from the hotel was located the Duma. This was like a parliament building where many political types gathered. There was no shortage of well-dressed, young clerks, interns and assistants walking about in the area.

On the fifth day, December 8th, I packed up my bags, said goodbye to the doorman and to Moscow, and headed for the airport. When I returned home to Houston, I learned that there had been a botched terrorist attack in Moscow. A woman had decided to make a statement of protest and had planned to blow up as many people as possible in the Duma.

On the morning of December 9, 2003, the Chechen terrorist attached an explosive belt around her waist and began walking toward the parliament building. The bomb apparently exploded prematurely. She had been approaching the Duma from around the corner where Hotel National was located. The bomb went off near the doorman and the Christmas tree where I stood each day. The doorman was killed. The Christmas tree and the glass front of the hotel were destroyed.

I missed the event by one day. Or, you could look at it the other way: the terrorist missed me by one day.

Story 24 – Stand Up (2015)

I have been playing sports, exercising and instructing others for decades. I teach Tae Kwon Do, train people with kettlebells, and run stretching and mobility classes. I offer both group classes and individual or private training sessions.

For several months, I had endured a small but nagging pain in my lower back on the right side. I tried all of the stretching and corrective exercises I could think of without success. A friend of mine had been to see an Airrosti practitioner and told me that this guy was great. Airrosti is a myofascial release system that is performed by specially trained chiropractors. I was curious about the system and signed up for several sessions with the Airrosti guy.

They guaranteed results in three sessions. Each session consisted of some specialized massage techniques to release the fascia, taping with kinesiotape, and foam rolling. After three sessions, nothing had changed. I felt better after each session, but the symptoms returned quickly. I liked the Airrosti guy and felt he was knowledgeable. So, I signed up for a few more sessions.

One session, after he had completed his myofascial work, he told me that my sacrum was out of alignment. He said that as an Airrosti practitioner he was no longer supposed to perform chiropractic adjustments but he felt that this would be beneficial. I agreed. So, my Airrosti guy (who is a very big man) twisted me up like a pretzel and then jumped onto my hips. As usual, after the kinesiotape and foam rolling, I felt better. This was on Tuesday.

Saturday morning I awoke early as usual. After all, I had a private session scheduled at 8:00 a.m. But, this morning was different. As I got out of bed I unpleasantly discovered that I couldn't stand up. My back hurt and I had an incredible pain and electrical sensation in my right leg. No matter what I did, I could not move into a fully erect position.

"No matter", I thought, "this will go away." So, I dressed, brushed my teeth, and headed to the gym. When I arrived, I vomited.

Against my strongest desires, I was forced to tell my client I was too sick to provide any private training. I sent him home and I tried to lie down. However, about every 30 minutes I was back in the restroom vomiting.

I thought all of this would pass eventually. Okay, I am a stubborn guy. After twenty-four hours of throwing up I told my wife that I had to go to the hospital.

The doctors gave me morphine and some drugs so that I would stop vomiting. They ran numerous tests, took x-rays, and did a CT scan. I was a mess and no longer really cared what they did.

The diagnoses finally came in. I had a compressed nerve in my lower back between L2 and L3. Emergency surgery on my back was planned for the next morning.

Now, I must say that, in general, I have strong objections to surgery on any back – especially *my* back. However, I was on morphine. I had severe pain. And, it felt like someone was running a high-voltage electrical current down my right leg. In short, I signed the consent documents and let them cut on me.

When I awoke, my right leg was no longer shaking and in spasms. This was a good sign. And, after a couple of days they sent me home to begin the recovery process.

I had lost ten percent of my bodyweight and I was incredibly weak. I discovered that I could not get off the ground and stand up without using both my hands for assistance.

I was very careful not to try to resume my strenuous activities to fast. I had been warned that a reoccurrence was possible if I overdid it. I began moving slowly and over time increased my load, my speed and my range of motion. After a period of a full year I am back to nearly one hundred percent.

This story illustrates just how fragile our *certain* realities are. It seems that we are absolutely sure what tomorrow morning will look like. We make plans and put them on the calendar. Yet, in the blink of an eye we may be unable to do even the simplest task. There are no guarantees yet we take most of our days for granted. It is only when we receive a wake up call, such as this one, that we truly appreciate that, once again, it wasn't yet our turn.

One More Story

Of course, there are many more stories of narrowly escaped mishaps. Many of them involve bars, nightclubs, alcohol and poor decisions. But, some bad situations were simply the result of getting lost or of being in the wrong place or an unfamiliar area at the wrong time. Every big city has areas that are best avoided late at night. Let's just say that I did not always make the wisest choices in these matters.

But luck, fate, and coincidence extend to much more than just injuries and life-or-death events. Much of my life's journey has been guided simply by changing personal goals or technological advances that have been made during my time here on this planet.

If you were born several hundred years ago and your last name was Miller, you were probably destined to be associated with grain preparation. Similarly, if your name was Taylor, your father and most people in your family were probably in the clothing business. People were trained when young and then they went to work. Their entire life's work was dedicated to the skill with which they were equipped after such apprenticeship. People were much less mobile. They tended to live their entire lives near their birthplace and local economies dictated that new jobs rarely appeared.

I believe I was very fortunate to have been born into an era where our economics and technology have been rapidly evolving. I have been able to explore a wide variety of hobbies, skills and careers. This makes me very happy since I never wanted to know exactly where I would be and what I would be doing twenty years into the future. Life is an adventure. Luckily for me, I have been able to take risks, learn new skills and reinvent myself with enthusiasm. I believe this ability to change roles will become ever more important to my children and future generations.

When I was in high school, I wanted to be a rock star. I wrote music for choir, band, musical productions, and the orchestra. But mostly I wanted to be on stage, making big bucks, playing jazz-rock music, and taking home the beautiful women. I was obsessed with this goal. I practiced, wrote music, played gigs and grew older. I learned along the way that the odds of becoming a star in the music business were astronomically small regardless of talent. There are thousands of extraordinarily gifted musicians who are still struggling to make a meager living. At the very old age of 25, I decided that I didn't want to look in the mirror at an old man of 30 and realize I had accomplished nothing in my life.

So, I changed directions. I returned to school to finish my undergraduate degree. I had a new goal. I would become a computer scientist and an electrical engineer. I would give up on my fantasy of stardom and settle down to do real, meaningful work.

After graduating from Rice University, my first job was working for a company called Intermetrics. The group I worked with developed software for the monitoring and control of oil tank farms. Our software showed the operators how much oil was in each tank and allowed them to move the oil from barges and trucks to and from the oil tanks.

We developed software in a language called Pascal and we worked on Texas Instruments computers. The type of computer was a TI-990 minicomputer. Now, this may sound like Greek to you, but to me, it was a fascinating and challenging job. I loved it. I truly became and expert in the programming language and in the TI-990 minicomputer. The year was 1984 and I was at the top of my game.

In 1986, the IBM personal computer was entering the workplace. And, more of interest to me, the TI-990 was officially declared obsolete by Texas Instruments. They introduced a new minicomputer that was completely unlike the TI-990 and incompatible with it. This meant that my immense knowledge, understanding and mastery of the TI-990 minicomputer were now rendered completely worthless.

So, I started my own company, Specialty Control Systems, and my plan was to develop similar software for monitoring and controlling oil tank farms, but *we* would use the IBM PC and the Microsoft DOS operating system. In those days, there was no pre-packaged software available for the IBM PC. If you wanted the PC to do something more than very poor word processing, you had to pay a software developer to write something. I had a new goal. I would be that guy. I would start over and become an expert on the IBM PC.

I worked very hard and learned the necessary programming languages, the IBM PC hardware, and the associated operating system. Once again I became an expert. And we successfully developed and sold several tank level monitoring systems. However, the IBM PC software market changed rapidly as everything related to computers had done for the past decade. Within the span of a few short years, pre-packed software began appearing on the market for nearly everything. I had charged $125 per hour for operating system support work on the TI-990 minicomputer. We had been charging $50 to $75 per hour for software developing services on the IBM PC. And, suddenly, users could purchase a "box" of software for $299 that had thousands of man-hours of development time in it. In short, no one wanted to pay us for software development. We were in no position to write elaborate software programs, package them in fancy boxes, and market them for less than a grand. The development and marketing would cost millions.

Next, the Microsoft DOS operating system was replaced by Microsoft Windows. And, the database management software that we had done our development in, Ashton-Tate's dBase III+, was now obsolete. We were forced to begin development in Microsoft's Visual FoxPro. Once again, skills, talents and expertise that were acquired with great difficulty were now useless relics.

Specialty Control Systems was struggling. We were now unable to be profitable by writing Tank Level Monitoring Systems. Fortunately, we were approached by Wolfenson Electric. They asked us to write a new accounting software package for them. This was a wonderful and surprising opportunity. But, I knew next to nothing about accounting systems and the associated computer software. Fortunately, Wolfenson Electric provided the training necessary for me to learn about standard accounting practices and Specialty Control Systems developed the software they required. In fact, at the time of this writing, much of the accounting software that was initially developed for Wolfenson Electric is still being used at Specialty Control Systems.

We sold a few of these new accounting packages. But, the computer world continued to change rapidly. Previously, programs ran on personal computers that were connected via a local area network to a file server. Now companies were migrating to cloud storage on wireless networks. Programs running on computers have been replaced with "apps" that run on smart phones or tablets.

Programmers now create "apps" or they focus on website development. The style of programming and the languages used are completely different. As a result, once again, all of the skills and expertise I have worked hard to acquire are obsolete.

Now, you might think that I am complaining about this. I am not. In fact, quite the opposite is true. I believe that we are most alive and energized when we are learning – when we are challenging ourselves to grow. Fortunately, changing technology has provided a clear motivation for me to continue to learn about new computer languages, hardware, and other advances. This helps keep me young.

It seems to me that this ever-changing world of computers and technology is becoming ever more volatile. New electronic hardware, software, programming languages, and other advances are appearing with greater frequency. And, these technological advances affect nearly all jobs in the workplace.

Take metalworking as an example. Many years ago metal was welded, filed and ground, polished, hammered, painted, and drilled. Then, additional machinery appeared that allowed heat treating, etching, lathing and electroplating. Now, computers control the lasers, the welding robots and the machining equipment that manufacture virtually everything from metal. The highest paid employees will be those who understand and can operate the current state-of-the-art computer-controlled equipment. And, as soon as the employee learns how this piece of equipment works, it will be updated or replaced with a cheaper, faster, and more advanced version.

I believe we can remain young as long as we challenge ourselves. We must learn new things to adequately stimulate our minds. And, we must likewise challenge our bodies. Efforts to increase our strength, stamina, speed and range of motion are required if we are to maintain a young and athletic body. I want to keep a functioning and quick mind and a youthful body because I love life, I have a terrific wife and I have two wonderful young boys. And, because it is not my turn.

Epilogue

The question you and I might ask ourselves is "Why am I still here?" The stories in this book have repeatedly, although indirectly, asked us this question. Are these simply coincidences? I sit here finishing up this manuscript during the Great Chinese Coronavirus Plague of 2020. Everyone is wondering what the health and economic impact of this disaster will be. Once again, life or fate is presenting challenges to me and all of humanity. There will be many deaths from this disease. There will also be massive job loss and many businesses will close. So, this is another excellent opportunity to ask ourselves, "What does this all mean?" Why are we struggling and what is the meaning of our lives?

It Doesn't Matter

The first and most nihilistic answer to this question is that it simply doesn't matter. There is no reason. We are born, we live, and then we die. Thousands of years and millions of lives lend some credence to this viewpoint. However, this explanation is simply not satisfying to me nor hopefully to you. I much prefer to believe that your life and my life are valuable things. If in fact life is just a game, then I prefer to play that game with enthusiasm and interest by assigning to it as much meaning as possible.

I find a similar objection to the view that there is no God — that we are only the accidental result of a series of wildly coincidental cosmic events. Matter coalesced and made the planets. Then, some extremely fortunate combination of sunlight, primordial soup and lightning occurred that caused the earliest forms of DNA to spontaneously erupt into being. From these early life forms, constant evolution encouraged amoeba to become fish. Fish then moved to land and evolved to become mankind.

Science may support much of this view of evolution. However, if this is the only explanation for the human species then we are purely an accident. We have no intrinsic value. And, we have no higher purpose to our role and our time on this earth. Were I to accept this viewpoint as is then nothing I could possibly do would have any meaning. So, for my own mental health and the continued appreciation of those around me I must attach value to my life and to the lives of others. Many people nowadays adhere to this solely, evolutionary theory and as a result bear the weight of its meaning. They believe that we mutated from some animal that evolved from some goop and therefore we have no purpose here. Could this be the explanation for the increasingly high rate of suicide, especially amongst young people?

Paradigm

As a child and as a young adult I had tons of drive and numerous goals. I went about working as hard as possible to achieve these aspirations. Much of what shapes our beliefs about the world and the dreams we hope to achieve in it come from our parents and our childhood environment. The adults in our lives tell us both what we must do and what we should desire. Our friends, relatives, schools and social environment also shape who we become and what we believe through the often inadvertent pressure they apply to us.

I believed I could accomplish anything when I was very young. I had no concept of my own mortality. I was also arrogant like many young people today. I believed that my education and my exceptional intellect were fully developed and that I *knew* what was right, what was wrong, and how the world worked. I was convinced that I was smarter than my parents. After all, they were really old – like in their forties.

Decades later, when I reached middle age, I realized that the paradigm of my youth was flawed. I had now acquired much more knowledge about the world, work, money, relationships, illness and death. I was no longer looking forward to finishing college and starting a career. I had experienced marriage albeit briefly. I began to question, even more deeply, the meaning of life. Answers were difficult to find.

More decades passed as I watched many people around me grow old and die. I began to question the value of accumulating wealth. People around me betrayed my friendship. My body was no longer as resilient as it had been. My worldview continued to change and evolve.

In hindsight, I can see that my paradigm had undergone significant changes during my life. These large changes were usually the result of many small modifications over an extended period. Now I have two young boys. (Yes, I started my family late in life.) There are clearly more changes ahead for me. Perhaps one of the meanings for my life is this journey of flexibility. We must often let go of the absolute certainty of what we know and adopt new paradigms. We must be willing to accept that what we absolutely know to be true may, in fact, be untrue or may only be our opinion.

Suffering

The Buddhist view of the world is that man's destiny is to suffer and all we can do is change our view of this suffering. While most of us currently live in an affluent society that is free from war and most diseases of poverty, this has not been the case for most of man's time on this planet. Constant fighting, widespread sickness, and famine often made life horrendous.

In this view, we are destined to endure illness, the tortures of weather, hunger and eventually death. However, I disagree that this is the purpose of life. In fact, there simply must be a significant and powerful reason for us to strive to survive and improve both our lives the lives of others. Without such motivation, the inevitable suffering of our lives would be unbearable.

Lessons

Life is always teaching me new lessons. For example, I learned that if I worked extremely hard I could build a successful business or acquire a new physical skill. Unfortunately, I also learned that if I spent too much time and attention on building a business or career to the exclusion of all else I might sacrifice my personal relationships. And, I learned that pushing my body too hard to acquire a physical talent without proper concern for stress reduction, nutrition, physical rehabilitation and rest the result could be chronic pain or injury.

There are myriad lessons to be learned. This is, to my way of thinking, the definition of wisdom. When one is willing to acknowledge the lessons that have been presented to him and thoughtfully reflect on what those lessons mean he could perhaps reach an old age and have the ability to evaluate problems using a much broader perspective. Perhaps the meaning of my life is to learn a few more lessons and work toward the integration of those data into a cohesive opinion. I have certainly gained greater respect for the knowledge and insight that mature people may hold.

It would be immodest for me to say I have acquired wisdom. But, I have learned a few things. Now, it seems it is time for me to share this knowledge with others. I have been studying Tae Kwon Do for nearly forty years. So, I now spend some of my time helping others develop the physical skills associated with this activity while hopefully sharing my love and enthusiasm for it. My first book, "Tae Kwon Do Essentials", was written to guide others to excellence in this sport.

I was fortunate enough to build a successful business. Many people asked how I did this. I responded to these inquiries by writing "From Manvel to Moscow" -- a book on the principles I followed during the formative years of this company.

Now, I am beginning a series of lectures on chronic pain and quality movement patterns. This work is a direct result of the years I have spent studying and teaching kettlebells, rehabilitative systems and the Z-Health system. For information on this amazing subject, you can

Each of these activities involve sharing the knowledge I have acquired with others. But, one thing I have realized during this process is that I must continue to study and learn new things if I am to have the ability to effectively pass on information. I read more now in order to refresh my knowledge and so that I can gain new perspectives on the material I *believe* I know and how to more effectively make this information available to others.

Sharing information with others and helping them improve their lives is something that excites me and brings me joy. I choose to believe that this is one of the reasons I am still here. I must continue to learn new things and I will improve my skills at sharing my acquired knowledge with others.

Society

My parents had little money. I started my first business on a shoestring budget working part time. After many years of hard work and sacrifice

I discovered that my business was profitable and I "suddenly" had significant income. Coming from a working class family I was somewhat ashamed that I was earning more money than my parents or siblings. After some soul searching I realized that earning more money primarily had one meaning – I now spent more money. Every time I purchased something, hired someone, or paid for a service I used some of my hard earned money. These actions support our nation's economy.

Money is not a static commodity. Even if I were to accumulate millions of dollars and put them in the bank, this would simply provide the bank with necessary resources to loan other people money. Similarly, money put into the stock market provides capital for businesses to invest in research, personnel or equipment.

Why do I care about this? I have had numerous employees over the past decades. Some of these individuals have worked hard for me for many years and I highly value them as friends. Were I to close my business they would lose their jobs. While our customers would certainly find other suppliers, they too have relied on my business, Specialty Control Systems. Customers and vendors form a relationship that is small part of a healthy economy.

Perhaps one of the reasons I am still here is this interactive economic community. Buying, selling, trading, helping, working, spending, and saving are all activities that support the people around us. I have been blessed to earn a lot of money and spend a lot of it. I will not take it with me. One of my personal missions is to remain energetic, enthusiastic, and engaged. The effect of this on the economy around me will be positive.

Family

I am on my third marriage. It would be an understatement to say that I am not proud of this statistical piece of information. But, I must own the details of my life. Divorce became easier and more widely accepted in the past 50 years. I sincerely meant it when I said to myself and the world around me, "until death do us part". But, more and more society was screaming at us to pursue our own inner dreams. Relationships, we have been told, are fluid and we should do whatever makes us happy. So, I buckled under the pressure and broke my vow.

I worked to the extreme and was too self-centered. In other words, my relationships were not at the top of my priority list. I now know that ignored relationships are very unlikely to flourish. Do this to your own peril. I don't believe I set out to deceive others. My loved ones were well aware of my drive and ambitions. But, when it comes to meaningful, long-term relationships, I have clearly been overly committed to numerous competing causes.

My current, most important and final wife is extremely smart and hard working. In many ways our personalities are similar. As a result, our relationship is always easy and positive. Not!

The relationship is more like a manic-depressive disorder. When we are both cooperative and in a good mood, everything is wonderful. However, when one of us is uncooperative, self-focused, or angry the other usually responds with a similar bad attitude. The result is less than desirable.

We have two young boys together. This development has changed my life. Now I have love for a couple of young people – the depth of which I could have never foretold. These kids are a kind of glue that holds my wife and me together.

But, even without the children, my love, respect and admiration for my wife are immense. I see myself in her. Not only do I see the good parts of me there, but I also see the unpleasant parts of me that for so many years I refused to acknowledge. I see her as a real partner – one with great qualities and with flaws. And, I appreciate that she holds up the mirror so that I can see myself more clearly. Perhaps my journey here is not yet complete because I have yet to acknowledge my relationship shortcomings and to master my own difficulties with anger and communication.

Children

My two boys have brought new joy into my life. I love watching them grow, learn and mature. I relish the fact that I get to play a part in this process. Of course, they learn a lot from their mother, their school, and their playmates.

They are constantly on my mind and I am trying to decipher the signals that our society is sending them, evaluating these messages, and deciding if and how I might intervene or add additional perspective to the noise.

My oldest boy is nine years old and has already begun asking me questions that I find very difficult to answer. He reminds me of how my mind was already questioning things when I was his age. For example, yesterday he asked me about the Christian faith. He wanted to know if the only way a Christian could get to heaven was to believe in Jesus. I told him yes – that Christians must believe that Jesus is the Son of God and that He died for our sins on the cross so that we would be saved.

Then he asked the hard question. So, we must believe this *before* we die? I said "Of course – before we die." He said he didn't understand because if we die and go to hell, then we will know for sure that we should have believed in Jesus and then we could go to heaven. Seems like some pretty good logic there.

I want my boys to think rationally and analytically and have the ability to apply deductive reasoning. As often as possible, I try to ask them questions that force them to use their minds in these ways.

As my boys grow and try to find their way through their young lives, I have a purpose. I have the opportunity to guide them on this journey. My life has meaning because I believe their lives have meaning.

Love

Many years ago, when I was probably six or seven years old, my grandmother became ill with cancer. I went to see her as she lay in bed waiting for the end. She was so happy to see me and I could see the joy that my presence brought her.

Unfortunately, there have been many relatives in my family who have died from cancer. My father died from COPD. All of these people knew they were dying. As they neared the end, I tried to spend time with each of them. I noticed that most people do not want to see someone on their deathbed. It is indeed a sad experience. But, I felt I must go. Why?

Two reasons. Firstly, when someone has reached the end of life, I felt that they probably didn't want to be alone. I wondered how I would feel were I to be in this position. I haven't obsessed about this, but I have thought about it. I don't want to die, but unlike in American fairy tales, where heroes live *happily ever after,* I am certain that I will. How do I want to die? I am pretty sure I don't want to know the answers to either the question "How" or "When". I simply want to live my life well and I hope the end is not a long, lingering period of intense suffering.

Secondly, I wanted to know what was important to my relatives as they neared death. I have always been curious about the meaning of life and I could sense that the things that are important change as we approach the end. If we spend our lives building a career and amassing a fortune, will that seem so important in the final moments. So, I wanted to ask a couple of questions. What did they see as the meaning of life and what was important to them now.

All of my friends and relatives shared similar views. In the end, the only thing that really matters is whom we love and who loves us. I believe that this is one of the main reasons why I am still here. There is still so much love to give!

www.ingramcontent.com/pod-product-compliance
Lightning Source LLC
Chambersburg PA
CBHW042331150426
43194CB00001B/23